A BOOK OF
PAGAN
RITUALS

A BOOK OF PAGAN RITUALS

Herman Slater
Editor

SAMUEL WEISER, INC.

York Beach, Maine

First published in one volume in 1978 by
Samuel Weiser, Inc.
Box 612
York Beach, ME 03910-0612

04 03 02 01 00 99 98
18 17 16 15 14 13 12

First published in two volumes in 1974 by Earth Religious Supplies

ISBN 0-87728-348-6
BJ

Printed in the United States of America

The paper used in this publication meets the minimum require-
ments of the American National Standard for Permanence of Paper
for Printed Library Materials Z39.48-1984.

CONTENTS

☆ ☆ ☆

The Pagan Way is, as Occultists put it, "On the right-hand path," and is devoted to the worship of that which is good in man and nature. Satanism, black magic and the like are actively opposed – we know that such cults are destructive in their effects and contrary to the evolutionary advance of humankind. The rituals of the Pagan Way cannot be twisted to harmful ways or purposes. Any attempt to do so would have very serious consequences for anyone who tried.

☆ ☆ ☆

PART ONE

BASIC PAGAN RITUALS

Introduction to Paganism

"Paganism? What's it all about?"

This question is being heard more frequently, here and abroad — for something very different has been quietly appearing on today's scene.

There are a lot of problems in the world today — wars, pollution, repression by one side or another, technology and commercialism gone mad, and far, far too many people. And it's getting worse.

Why?

What has caused the cascading insanity that we see around us? More importantly, what can we grasp onto which is secure and *worth* believing?

Some of us think we know why this has all happened; if you're interested and concerned, you, too, may eventually realize why things have turned out this way. (More on this subject later).

The important thing is to get back, in some small way, to the mental and spiritual outlook which can make this nightmare world, and all its problems, quite unnecessary.

It can be done — our distant ancestors knew how. They knew how to live *with* nature, to understand the reasons behind it. They had a basic knowledge of the balance which is a part of everything — something we have lost in the centuries and millenia that have passed.

But not lost irretrievably, for it is with us again. It is a faith and a way of living.

It is Paganism.

Why Now?

Paganism is returning to the world!

Really, though, it had never left — for folk beliefs and the ancient Witch cult have always been with us. But for the past several centuries folk wisdom was given a Christian overlay and largely ignored; the Witches, with their age-old lore, were forced underground by persecution — with much loss to the common man.

Now the established major religions are greatly weakened and tottering, their foundations largely destroyed by a rapidly changing world. Their efforts to adjust and alter, to "keep step with the times," have only weakened them further. Only the prop of being socially convenient has kept the churches from total collapse. And the structure of society itself is weakening, with "social convenience" having less and less power as a new generation increasingly scorns that which is useless and irrelevant.

Science itself, starting with Galileo and others as a reaction to a stale and oppressive religious establishment, seems to have reached a plateau in its discoveries. New research has become increasingly expensive, and the feeling is growing that the results gained are now justifying less and less of the cost put into them. Political pressures fashion the wonders of science into weapons which are both cruel and fearsome. Commercialism, in its mindless striving for money, has managed to prostitute the finest technical developments and with their wastes to pollute much of what still remains of the natural world.

Politics has reached a similar impasse. Both Marxism and Capitalism were created using the precepts of Christianity, and thus both suffer from the same weaknesses as their parent: inflexibility, dogma, intolerance and hypocrisy. Those who have lived under both systems say that Marxism is considerably more drab and mechanistic than its rival. Thus we can expect that the current intellectual fashions tending toward Marx will ultimately be halted by the dull, hard wall of reality.

But then — where else will there be to go?

The answer lies deep within ourselves — where it has always been — and out in the world of nature, where it has long waited.

For the Pagan Way is very close to the soul of humanity; it is a natural belief which sees man as he is, and the world as it is, and seeks to push neither into a preconceived mold. Further, Paganism sees the mystery and richness of nature, and opens the way to an understanding of it which the modern world has overlooked.

The Pagan Way, as it now exists, is based on valid beliefs from the distant past. The present store of rituals and practices has been drawn from ancient sources, restored and updated by scholars from various Pagan groups, existing but never advertised, whose traditions stretch unbroken since far before the dawn of history.

There is much flexibility here, for Paganism is not fixed and dogmatic. There are new adventures of the mind and spirit, for Paganism thrives on joy, beauty and color.

And there is the inspiration of working toward a new world — one totally different from today.

And one far better.

What is Paganism?

Paganism recognizes that throughout all things — from the atom to the universe — there is a duality. Night and day, love and hate — the ancient Oriental concept of Yin and Yang which was long matched by similar concepts in what we now call Europe.

The Pagan realizes that there is no heaven except that which he himself makes, and likewise no hell but that of his own creation.

Most Pagans believe that they have experienced previous lives in previous eras of this world. And they can point to impressive evidence backing them up.

A Pagan refuses to believe that mankind is born innately sinful, and realizes that the concept of "sin" is itself arbitrary and hurtful to human nature.

The Pagan knows that man is not better than woman, nor woman superior to man. What one lacks the other can give, and one cannot be truly alive without the other! There is no greater magic than that of man and woman together.

A Pagan knows that what is called "magic" does truly exist, and it is often worked by those who are in touch with certain forces of the natural world

The Pagan believes that what cannot be seen is of the greatest importance — that much exists of which the present world's science knows little or nothing. And that anyone can experience what is normally considered to be beyond "reality."

Paganism has a deep love for things natural and wild, as it knows that there are many beings which are intelligent and wise — and not all human. Yet they may be met in places of seclusion and wilderness by those who earnestly desire to know them — and it is for this reason that the Pagan does not allow his or her heart and mind to become cluttered by the useless trivia of a commercial-technical society.

A Pagan knows that there are deep forces and tides which underlie all things, and that there exist here on earth infinitely complex multidimensional matrices of living power which are far beyond the capability of a human to understand. That there is intelligence here and the greatest of wisdom — for such has always existed and always will.

The Pagan realizes that mankind has always known of the existence of this Supernal Intelligence, and has called It by thousands of names for tens of thousands of years. That men and women of all eras have drawn strength and power, warmth and security from this source — at times in ways which would seem to transcend reality!

iii

Paganism teaches that the Highest source is both female and male in its aspects and that, though vastly beyond our capacity to understand, we can perceive It — or Them — as individuals, or as Goddess and God to whom we can speak, and receive answers.

The Pagan knows that over the past two or three thousand years humankind has stressed a narrow portion of the God in his religions and ignored or denied the role of the Goddess — with the result that history has come to be a chronicle of disasters. A balance is needed, with perhaps a greater stress on the Goddess (right *now*) in Her many aspects, to restore peace and to assure a meaningful survival of ourselves and our descendants.

This is Paganism!

Pagan Musing

We're of the old religion, sired of Time, and born of our beloved Earth Mother. For too long the people have trodden a stony path that goes only onward beneath a sky that goes only upwards. The Horned God plays in a lonely glade, alone, for the people are scattered in this barren age, and the winds carry his plaintive notes over deserted heaths and reedy moors and into the lonely grasses! Who knows now the ancient tongue of the Moon? And who speaks still with the Goddess? The magic of the land of Lirien and the old pagan gods have withered in the dragon's breath; the old ways of magic have slipped into the well of the past, and only the rocks now remember what the moon told us long ago, and what we learned from the trees, and the voices of the grasses and the scents of flowers.

We're pagans and we worship the pagan gods, and among the people there are witches yet who speak with the moon and dance with the Horned One. But a witch is a rare pagan in these days, deep and inscrutable, recognisable only by her own kind — by the light in her eyes and the love in her breast, by the magic in her hands and the lilt of her tongue and by her knowledge of the real.

The Wiccan way is one path. There are many; there are pagans the world over who worship the Earth Mother and the Sky Father, the Rain God and the Rainbow Goddess, and the Little People in the mists on the other side of the vale. A pagan is one who worships the goddesses and gods of nature, whether by observation or by study, whether by love or

1

admiration, or whether in their sacred rites with the Moon, or the great festivals of the Sun.

Many suns ago, as the pale dawn of reason crept across the pagan sky, man grew out of believing in the gods . . . he has yet to grow out of disbelieving in them. He who splits the Goddess on an existence-nonexistence dichotomy will earn himself only paradoxes, for the gods are not so divided and neither are the lands of the Brother of Time. Does a mind exist? Ask her and she will tell you yes, but seek her out, and she'll elude you. She is in every place, and in no place, and you'll see her works in all places, but herself in none. Existence was the second-born from the Mother's womb and contains neither the first-born nor the unborn. Show us your mind, and we'll show you the gods! No matter that you can't, for we can't show you the gods. But come with us and the Goddess herself will be our love and the God will call the tune. A brass penny for your reason! For logic is a closed ring, and the child doesn't validate the Mother, nor the dream the Dreamer. And what matter the wars of opposites to she who has fallen in love with a whirlwind, or to the lover of the arching rainbow?

But tell us of your Goddess as you love her and the gods that guide your works and we'll listen with wonder, for to do less would be arrogant. But we'll do more; for the heart of man is aching for memories only half forgotten, and the Old Ones, only half unseen. We'll write the old myths as they were always written, and we'll read them on the rocks and in the caves and in the deep of the greenwood's shade, and we'll hear them in the rippling mountain streams and in the rustling of the leaves, and we'll see them in the storm clouds, and in the evening mists. We've no wish to create a new religion . . . for our religion is as old as the hills and older, and we've no wish to bring differences together. Differences are like different flowers in a meadow, and we are all one in the Mother.

What need is there for a pagan movement, since our religion has no teachings and we hear it in the wind and feel it in the stones and the moon will dance with us as she will? There is a need. For long the Divider has been among our people, and the tribes are no more. The sons of the Sky Father have all but conquered nature, but they have poisoned her breast and the Mother is sad . . . for the songbirds, the fish, and the butterflies are dying. And the night draws on. A curse on the conquerors! But not of us, for they curse themselves . . . for they are of nature, too. They have stolen our magic and sold out to the mindbenders and the mindbenders tramp a maze that has no outlet . . . for they fear to go down into the dark waters, and they fear the real for the One who guards the path.

Where are the pagan shrines? And where do the people gather? Where is the magic made? And where are the Goddess and the Old Ones? Our shrines are in the fields and on the mountains, and in the stars, the wind, deep in the greenwood and on the algal rocks where two streams meet. But the shrines are deserted, and if we gathered in the arms of the Moon for our ancient rites to be with our gods as we were of old we would be stopped by the dead who now rule the Mother's land and claim rights of ownership on the Mother's breast, and make laws of division and frustration for us. We can no longer gather with the gods in a public place and the old rites of communion have been driven from the towns and cities ever deeper into the heath where barely a handful of heathens have remained to guard the old secrets and enact the old rites. There is magic in the heath far from the cold grey society, and there are islands of magic hidden in the entrails of the metropoles behind closed doors. But the people are few, and the barriers between us are formidable. The Old Religion has become a dark way; obscure, and hidden in the protective bosom of the night. Thin fingers turn the pages of a book of shadows while the sunshine seeks in vain his worshippers in his leafy glades.

Here, then, is the basic reason for a Pagan Way; we must create a pagan society wherein everyone shall be free to worship the goddesses and gods of nature. The relationship between a worshipper and her gods shall be sacred and inviolable, provided only that in the love of one's own gods, one does not curse the names of the gods of others.

It's not yet our business to press the law-makers with undivided endeavor to unmake the laws of repression and, with the Mother's love, it may never become our business . . . for the stifling tides of dogmatism are at last in ebb. Our first work and our greatest wish is to come together, to be with each other in our tribes . . . for we haven't yet grown from the Mother's breast to the stature of gods. We're of the earth, and kin to all the children and impoverished of the old genetic pool. The Red Child lives yet in America; the old Australians are still with their nature gods; the Black Child has not forsaken the gods; the Old Ones still live deep in the heart of Mother India, and the White Child has still a foot on the old Wiccan way; but Neanderthaler is no more and her magic faded as the Lli and the Archan burst their banks and the ocean flowed in to divide the isle of Erin from the Land of the White Goddess.

Man looked with one eye on a two-faced god when he reached for the heavens and scorned the Earth which alone is our life and our provider and the bosom to which we have ever returned since the dawn of time. He who looks only to reason to plumb the unfathomable is a fool, for logic is an echo already implicit in the question, and it has no voice of its own; but he is no greater fool than he who scorns logic or derides its impotence from afar . . . and fears to engage in fair combat when he stands upon opponent's threshold. Don't turn your back on Reason, for his thrust is deadly; but confound him and he'll yield . . . for his code of combat is honorable. So here is more of the work of Paganism. Our lore has become encrusted over the ages with occult trivia and the empty vaporings of the lost. The occult arts are in a state of extreme decadence; alien creeds oust our native arts and, being as little understood as our own forgotten arts, are just as futile for their lack of understanding, and more so for their unfamiliarity. Misunderstanding is rife. Disbelief is black on every horizon, and vampires abound on the blood of the credulous. Our work is to reject the trivial, the irrelevant and the erroneous, and to bring the lost children of the Earth Mother again into the court of the Sky Father where reason alone will prevail. Belief is the deceit of the credulous; it has no place in the heart of a pagan.

But while we are sad for those who are bemused by Reason, we are deadened by those who see no further than his syllogisms as he turns the eternal wheel of the Great Tautology. We are not fashioned in the mathematician's computations, and we were old when the first alchemist was a child. We have walked in the magic forest, bewitched in the old Green Things; we have seen the cauldron and the one become many and the many in the one; we know the Silver Maid of the moonlight and the sounds of the cloven feet. We have heard the pipes on the twilight ferns, and we have seen the spells of the Enchantress, and Time stilled. We have been into the eternal darkness where the Night Mare rides and rode her to the edge of the Abyss and beyond, and we know the dark face of the Rising Sun. Spin a spell of words and make a magic knot; spin it on the magic loom and spin it with the gods. Say it in the old chant and say it to the Goddess, and in her name. Say it to a dark well and breathe it on a stone. There are no signposts on the untrod way, but we will make our rituals together and bring them as our gifts to the Goddess and her God in the great rites.

Here, then, is our work in the Pagan Way; to make magic in the name of our gods, to share our magic where the gods would wish it: and to come together in our ancient festivals of birth, and life, of death and of change in the old rhythm. We will print the rituals that can be shared in the written word; we will do all in our power to bring the people together, to teach those who would learn, and to learn from those who can teach, we will initiate groups, bring people into groups, and groups to other groups in our common devotion to the Goddesses and Gods of nature. We will not storm the secrets of any coven, nor profane the tools, the magic, and still less, the gods of another.

We will collect the myths of the ages, of our people and of the pagans of other lands, and we will study the books of the wise and we will talk to the very young. And whatever the pagan needs in her study, or her worship, then it is our concern and the business of the Pagan Way to do everything possible to help each other in our worship of the gods we love.

We are committed with the lone pagan on the seashore, with he who worships in the fastness of a mountain range or she who sings the old chant in a lost valley far from the metalled road. We are committed with the wanderer, and equally with the prisoner, disinherited from the Mother's milk in the darkness of the industrial wens. We are committed, too, with the coven, with the circular dance in the light of the full moon, with the great festivals of the sun, and with the gatherings of the people. We are committed to build our temples in the towns and in the wilderness, to buy the lands and streams from the landowners and give them to the Goddess for her children's use, and we will replant the greenwood as it was of old for love of the dryad stillness, and for love of our children's children.

When the streams flow clear and winds blow pure, when the sun never more rises unrenowned nor the moon rides in the skies unloved; when the stones tell of the Horned God and the greenwood grows deep to call back her own ones, then our work will be ended and the Pagan Way will return to the beloved womb of our old religion . . . to the nature goddesses and gods of paganism.

4

Altar Arrangement

The following arrangement of the central altar is used at many Pagan rituals:

NORTH

Wand

Earth
Symbol

| WEST | Water
Symbol | **GODDESS
SYMBOL** | Air
Symbol | EAST |

Fire
Symbol

SOUTH

The various symbols are usually as follows:

     EARTH: Rich loam in an earthenware cup, inscribed with a pentacle in the bottom.

     AIR: Incense placed in an earthenware cup and burned during the rite.

FIRE: Vegetable oil in an earthenware cup with a floating wick which is lit during the rite. Or a candle placed in an earthen cup.

WATER: Pure water in an earthenware cup.

Substitutions may be made if it is preferable.

The wand should, if possible, be a thirteen-inch willow rod. If it is desired, the wand may be polished, painted black, and tipped with silver. But even a rough, unfinished one would be satisfactory.

Candles may be placed at either side of the Goddess Symbol or before it.

Notes on Rituals

The rites of Paganism are held at the following times:
>Samhain (October 31)
>Lady Day (February 2)
>First Day of Spring (March 21)
>May Day (May 1)
>First Day of Summer (June 21)
>August Eve (August 1)
>First Day of Fall (September 21)
>Yule (First day of Winter, or Dec. 24-25)

Music is often used in Pagan rites. A very wide variety of music may be used, the only requirement being that it feel proper and appropriate to those taking part in the rituals.

When a ritual is underway, it is best not to leave the circle or the area in which the rite is being performed.

A woman should at all times strive to be more of a woman; a man should at all times strive to be more of a man. Each should always aid the other.

Each grove, or each pagan who possesses a copy of this material should always endeavor to add spells, rituals, and other lore which can be useful.

Each rite may be altered and amended as the people see fit, bearing in mind that the *intent*, rather than the specific word, is of most importance.

Beware of charlatans and frauds, and warn others of them. True Pagans, like true witches, do not feel it necessary to trumpet to the world of their fame, and to expand their own feelings of self-importance that they may impress others. Neither will a true pagan or true witch ask money for teaching of lore, performance of rites, or the working of magic, though small gifts of thanks might at times be accepted.

The compulsive seeking of money beyond that which is necessary, like the striving for power over one's fellow humans, is a sickness of the mind and should be handled as such.

☆ ☆ ☆

Pagan Ritual for General Use

A circle should be marked on the floor, surrounding those who will participate in the ceremony. An altar is to be set up at the center of the circle. At the center of the altar shall be placed an image of the Goddess, and an incense burner placed in front of it. Behind the image should be a wand fashioned from a willow branch. Candles should be set upon the altar ... a total of five, since one is to be set at each quarter and one will remain on the altar during the rite.

When all of the people are prepared they shall assemble within the circle. The woman acting as priestess shall direct the man who acts as priest to light the candles and incense. She shall then say:

> The presence of the noble Goddess
>   extends everywhere
> Throughout the many strange,
>   magical,
> And beautiful worlds
> To all places of wilderness,
>   enchantment, and freedom.

She then places a candle at the North and pauses to look outward, saying:

> The Lady is awesome.
> The powers of death bow before Her.

The person closest to the East takes a candle from the altar and places it at that quarter, saying:

> Our Goddess is a Lady of Joy.
> The winds are Her servants.

The person closest to the South takes a candle from the altar
and places it at that quarter, saying:

> Our Goddess is a Goddess of Love.
> At Her blessing and desire
> The sun brings forth life anew.

The person closest to the West takes a candle from the altar
and places it at that quarter, saying:

> The seas are the domains of our
>   Serene Lady
> The mysteries of the depths are Hers
>   alone.

The priest now takes the wand, and starting at the North,
draws it along the entire circle clockwise back to the north
point, saying:

> The circle is sealed, and all herein
> Are totally and completely apart
> From the outside world,
> That we may glorify the Lady whom
>   we adore.
> Blessed Be!

ALL REPEAT: **Blessed Be!**

The priest now holds the wand out in salute toward the
North for a moment and then hands it to the priestess, who
also holds it out in salute. She motions to the group to repeat
the following lines after her:

> As above, so below . . .
> As the Universe, so the soul.
> As without, so within.
> Blessed and gracious one,

On this day do we consecrate to you
Our bodies,
Our minds,
And our spirits,
Blessed Be!

Now is the time for discussion and teaching. Wine and light refreshments may be served. When the meeting has ended all will stand and silently meditate for a moment. The priestess will then take the wand and tap each candle to put it out, starting at the north and going clockwise about the circle, while saying:

Our rite draws to its end.
O lovely and gracious Goddess,
Be with each of us as we depart.

The circle is broken!

Cauldron Rite

Construct a circle large enough for all members of the group. At the center of the circle should be built an altar of ash, birch, and willow, formed into a pyramid. Each of the three sticks should be as long as the priestess is tall. They should be bound at the top with flax or wool yarn colored green with a natural dye. Hanging from the center of the three woods will be the cauldron, and sitting on top of the "broome" will be a large sphere of glass or crystal.

The perimeter of the circle should be sprinkled with chalk and with the ash from the previous fire used in the rite. Incense should be burned within the area to assist in creating the proper atmosphere. The number of pots of incense should be the number of the Goddess invoked (see below). Beneath the cauldron a fire will be lit, and continuously fed throughout the rite as needed. The cauldron itself should be no more than half full of water, and much calendala, ivy, and laurel (if possible) added to it.

A procession of the worshippers will be led to the circle by the priestess and her consort. When she and he enter the circle they will begin a dance about the circle clockwise. The priestess will lead, with the priest's hands upon her hips, and the next person's hands on his, etc., forming a chain . . . as much as possible alternating male and female. The dance around the ring will form a spiral and the members will go around the number of the Goddess to be invoked. That is, for the Maiden = 3×3; the Mother = 6×3; and the Crone = 9×3.

While turning about the circle in the dance the members should imagine the love force of life entering their bodies from their bare feet and spiralling slowly upward to the head, in a clockwise motion. This spiral should be timed to reach the head when the dance is completed. When the dance is stopped each will be facing the "broome" and will gaze into the sphere. Here instead of keeping your hands on the next person's hips, move closer together and put your arms around the next person's waist, thus making a complete connected circle.

This is the point of inspiration, and those called to pray will voice the poetry expressed, as each feels drawn to do so. Usually in a group it is best to silently voice the invocation, although if it is a group whose members are well-attuned to each other the voicing aloud can have a powerful effect. This is the point of mysticism and magic and the inspiration of the Lady . . . and at this point one feels as if one is near a great bell or drum which is tolling out and vibrating the mind and soul until they become one with the Goddess. It is at this point that you should make your desires known to the Goddess with great hope of their being fulfilled . . . for you are one with Her!

When this portion of the rite is done, and all will instinctively know when one's private meditations are completed, the more routine aspects of a meeting may take place. A feast of bread, wine, cheese, and whatever has been brought can be eaten, and during this time the priestess or priest will give instructions in the devotion to the Goddess and God, and each present may tell of his experiences. This "party" will last as long as necessary, with joy and love and true happiness being the order throughout.

At the end of the ceremony, or feast, all will rise, again arm-about-waist, and slowly turn about the circle the number of the Lady invoked. At the last turn the rite ends, though probably the closeness that the people will feel for each other will prevent immediate dispersal.

Rite of Purification

Prior to the start of the ceremony a circle shall be inscribed on the floor, being large enough to easily accommodate all who will be participating. The altar shall be set with a symbol of the Goddess at its center, and the symbols of the four elements placed about it. Thirteen candles shall be placed on the altar prior to the start, and a cauldron (or other suitable container) of pure, cold water placed before the altar. A wand, preferably a thirteen-inch rod of willow, shall be brought into the circle by the priestess.

To begin the rite all shall gather within the circle, each carrying a cup or goblet. The priestess shall direct the priest to light the first candles, and those others within the circle to light the rest. As each does so, she or he shall say:

> **In thy Name, blessed Lady,**
> **Do I build a part**
> **Of this magical circle.**

The priest shall place the first candle at the north point of the circle. Afterwards, under the direction of the priestess, each person shall place another candle at the edge of the circle, working in a clockwise direction. As each does place a candle, the above invocation shall be repeated. When all candles have been placed there should be twelve evenly-spaced about the circle and one on the altar before the symbol of the Goddess.

When the circle has thus been set, the priestess shall face to the east with the wand raised in her right hand, and say:

> **O blessed Lady of the Willow,**
> **Of things wild and free**
> **We do ask for your presence**
> **And for your blessing**

Within this circle,
For the rites which
We shall perform.

She shall then give the wand to the priest, who shall similarly offer a salute.

The priestess and priest shall hold their hands over the cauldron in an attitude of blessing, and say:

PRIEST: May this water, clear and fresh,
Cleanse the soul and the spirit
As, in symbol,
It does cleanse the hands.

PRIESTESS: May our Lady
Grant peace, and healing
And purity of soul
To us all.

BOTH: **Blessed Be!**

All paired, man with woman (insofar as it is possible) within the circle, the priest shall proclaim:

I do charge you all,
In the name of our Lady,
To wash away that
Which does stain the soul
And the spirit

All shall kneel at the edge of the circle in pairs of men and women. In turn, each shall slowly pour water over the outstretched hands of the other, reaching out over the edge of the circle, saying:

In the Name of the Goddess
I do cleanse thee, my friend.

When one is finished, she or he will ritually cleanse the other, as above. When all are finished, the priestess shall say to all:

Place your cups at the edge of the
    circle,
And come join with me, saying as I do
    say.

All shall repeat as the priestess says:

O Lady of the Streams and Lakes
    And of water pure and sweet,
We do ask for your blessings
For we are your children.
Bring us closer, we do ask
To the pure and free world of nature.
Banish guilt forever,
And show us new paths of
    understanding.
Lead us ever into your world
Of mystery, wonderment, and
    beauty.
Blessed Be!

If there are other activities to be accomplished they shall be done at this time, with the approval of the priestess ... such as light refreshments, singing, exercises in meditation, teaching, and the like.

When all is finished the priestess or priest shall direct each one within the circle to take the wand and use it to tap out the candles, working clockwise from the north as before. Each shall say:

> In your Name, Gracious One,
> Do I dissolve away
> A part of this circle.

When the last candle is out the priestess shall hold the wand out in salute toward the west and state:

> This circle is ended.
> All power to the Goddess!

ALL REPEAT: **All power to the Goddess!**

The Circle of Divination

The altar shall be set up in the usual way, but with three candles on the altar itself. Light refreshments may be placed nearby for use during the ceremony. The items used for divination are placed on the altar.

Four candles will be placed before the altar at the start. (Earthenware lamps, or earthen cups with oil and floating wicks, may be used if desired.)

This rite is useful for any type of augury or scrying: tarot, crystal, mirror, cauldron-scrying, palmistry, ouija, lithomancy, rune-casting, and many others. The teaching of divination is also best done within this circle.

A circle shall be drawn on the floor which is large enough for all to relax therein, since this is an informal rite. When all are within the circle, the woman who acts as priestess will light the candles and incense, saying:

> Our friends of the night,
> Of mist, and of moonlight . . .
> You who are seldom seen.
> Be with us now
> And spread apart the veil of Being
> That we may look beyond.

She then has the man who acts as priest take the four candles from before the altar and place them at the west, the north, the east, and the south points of the circle in that order.

When this is done she will direct four of those within the circle to present the symbols of the elements to the four quarters . . . if possible the persons chosen should be among those who will be performing divination later in the rite.

The one chosen to present the air symbol shall take it from the altar and stand, holding it out toward the north, the east, the south, and the west, saying:

17

O elementals of the water
Hearken to your sign.
Open the windows of Where and
When,
And let us see beyond.

The same should be done and said for earth, air, and fire.
The priestess then holds the wand out in salute toward the
south, invoking:

O Queen of magic and silence,
We have gathered the sprites of
nature
To help us delve into that
which lies beyond.
We ask that you make strong and
keen
Our inner eyes
As we search through the veil,
And let only influences which are
good
Enter within the circle.
This rite is yours, oh Lady of
Mystery.
Be with us, we ask.
Blessed Be!

ALL: Blessed Be!

Now is the time for relaxation and the various forms of
divination. The priestess and priest, or others, will aid,
guide, and teach as necessary. Light refreshments may be
served.

When it is judged that the rite should end, the priest shall
stand with wand outstretched in salute and say:

We do thank all who have
Been with us here . . .
Those whom we can see,
And those who are not of this world
And we thank the Blessed One.

He shall direct those nearest the candles at the four quarters to put them out. Then he shall put out the lights on the altar, saying:

The ritual is done!
Blessed Be!

ALL: **Blessed Be!**

Rites of Healing

(The following rituals are done primarily for practice, to develop the talents of healing, and are performed with volunteers.)

When healing is not practical through normal medical means or by application of herbal cures the Healing Ritual may be conducted.

To begin, the woman who acts as priestess lights the two candles on the altar, lights the incense, then lights thirteen candles which have been placed before the altar. The person who is ill shall sit on a chair at the middle of the room, facing the altar though not near it. The priest, or the healer, will place the thirteen candles about the ill one.

I. WITH HEALER

The healer shall stand before the priestess at the altar. Touching the hands of the healer with the wand the priestess shall say:

> **I do charge you**
> **In the name of Our Lady of Healing**
> **And through Her power**
> **To heal, to put aright the body,**
> **And give release from pain.**
> **Blessed Be.**

HEALER: **Blessed Be!**

The healer stands next to the ill one, holding his or her hands just over the afflicted part or area, though the healer's hands do not quite touch the person being healed. The healer shall say:

I do ask,
In the names of the Old Gods,
That pure life-force
Be drawn through me
And out from these hands
Into that which must be healed.
To remain and to strengthen
Until all is well.

The healer is to remain in this position until the feeling is received that the work of healing is accomplished.

II. HEALING BY GROUP

If the ill one is male, the priestess shall guide the group; if the healing must be done for a woman the priest shall guide the group. All of the group shall sit just outside the candles. The priestess or priest will explain to all the nature of the healing to be done. Then, taking a candle and holding it aloft, shall say:

I do charge you
In the name of Our Lady of Healing
And through Her power
To heal, to put aright the body,
And give release from pain.
Blessed Be!

ALL: Blessed Be!

The priestess or priest then stands beside the ill one, holding the candle in front of the subject's eyes, slightly above, and about one and one-half feet away. The priestess or priest shall then say:

Now as you gaze steadily
At this simple flame,
Seeing only its light,
All those about the circle
Shall concentrate steadily
On your healing.
All who sit about
The circle of candles,
Hear me and do as I say . . .
Look closely at the one who is ill
And picture clearly the pure
    life-force
Flowing from all who sit here
Strong and powerful . . .
Into the afflicted body.
There to remain and to strengthen
Until healing is done.

The priestess or priest, and all the rest, shall remain in concentration without moving until the priestess or priest feels that the healing has been done, closing the rite by saying:

The rite of healing
Is finished!

Those nearest the various candles shall put them out.

Other means of healing may be used within this basic ritual.

The work of healing is cumulative: that which is done will stay with the ill one and quietly continue working. In a few cases, however, it may be necessary to use several sessions of healing.

The Eight Grove Festivals

I. SAMHAIN

If a meal is served on the evening of this rite, it should include pork, apples, and wine. If possible, three small sheaves of corn or grain should be set about the place of worship.

To begin, incense should be lit. Herb incenses are best at this season, such as nutmeg, dried mint, heliotrope, etc. Five candles are placed about an image of the Goddess at the center of the ritual area. Three candles (white, red, and black) represent the Goddess, the fourth candle is white to symbolize the hearth, and the fifth is red to stand for the season. A plate of small bread balls, one for each person present, is placed near the center, as is a small dish of salt. An earthenware cup half filled with wine should be placed near the image, and all arranged pleasingly. A dim red lamp may be lit to symbolize the God in his death-aspect of this season. All who are present should sit or kneel in a circle, leaving some space at the center about the image and other items. Three women are chosen to act as priestesses in this ritual ... the youngest being the maiden-priestess, the older the mother-priestess, and the eldest the crone-priestess.

The crone-priestess lights the candles about the image, saying:

> Three candles we light
> For the Goddess ...
> As Maiden, as Mother, as Crone.
> The candle of the hearth we light
> For hearth-flames belong to Her.
> Now with the hearth-candle
> We do relight the taper of red ...
> As we light the winter's fires
> In this place sacred to Her.

The man chosen to be priest sits before the wine goblet, pauses, and says:

> **This is a time that is not a time**
> **In a place that is not a place**
> **On a day that is not a day**
> **Between the worlds**
> **And beyond . . .**

He pauses for the space of thirteen heartbeats, then placing his hands over the wine in an attitude of blessing, he says:

> **Blessed be this wine, and this bread**
> **With the life of the years**
> **And the deep love of the Goddess.**
> **Blessed Be!**

ALL: **Blessed Be!**

The maiden, mother, and crone priestesses take up the salt dish, the bread plate, and the wine cup respectively. Starting within the western part of the circle they offer each person a piece of bread, salt to dip it in, and a dedicational sip of wine.

The mother offers bread, saying softly:

> **May you have sufficiency.**

The Maiden offers the salt:

> **May you have good health.**

The crone offers the cup of wine:

May your spirit be strong.

When all have partaken, the priest distributes glasses and wine, and explains some of the significance of the Samhain festival. He then opens the rite for any to participate who so desire. Scrying and divination by crystal, black mirror, tarot, runes, pendulum, planchette, and such are traditional at this rite.

When all is finished the mother-priestess shall put out the candles, saying:

> **Though these flames**
> **Of the material world**
> **Be darkened,**
> **They shall ever burn**
> **In the worlds beyond.**
> **The rite is ended.**
> **Merry meet, merry part!**

ALL: **Merry meet, merry part!**

II. YULE

A Yule-tree shall be set up and decorated, with lights and all trimmings, in the northern part of the ritual area. In the southern part the altar shall be arranged as usual, except that behind the altar (or at the back of it) should be placed a log of oak with thirteen candles of various colors affixed to it. A candle-holder should be fitted with three or five candles which are white, and the holder placed before the altar. For the meal which follows this rite it is traditional to serve some kind of pork, or to prepare a cake in the shape of a boar.

For this ritual the women taking part should, if possible,

wear long robes or gowns of varying colors. A man shall be chosen to act as priest and three women of varying age selected to be priestesses. The youngest shall be the maiden-priestess; she should wear white, if possible. The next shall be the mother-priestess; she should wear red, if possible. The oldest shall be the crone-priestess; she should wear black and have a veil, if possible.

To begin the crone-priestess sits or stands at the west. All who are in the rite do take up candles. The priest lights the tree, the incense, and the candles before and behind the altar. The mother-priestess stands before the tree and says to the group:

> In this, the Season of the White God-
> dess,
> Do we celebrate the festival of Yule:
> The rebirth of the sun,
> And of life for the coming year.
> This eternal cycle
> Do we mark here.

The maiden-priestess takes the candle-holder and holds it while the priest lights it for her. He then lights the candles of all others. The Maiden, the Mother and the priest then lead a slow procession three times clockwise about the ritual area, stopping finally with the Maiden standing before the crone-priestess. All do gather about, as the maiden-priestess says:

> The tides are changing, O crone.
> I come to claim
> That which now is mine.

The crone-priestess takes off her veil; the mother-priestess take it and places it on the maiden-priestess as the crone-priestess says:

The days grow longer, and the sun is
   reborn.
My season is past, but yours is yet to
   come.
Take well the counsel of the years,
But be wise and bold in your own
   actions
I do bid you.

The maiden-priestess then says to her:

I do thank you, wise one.
Your grace in ceding to me
Shall be rewarded.

The maiden-priestess then stands before the tree and
holds her candelabrum high aloft, saying to all:

All does change
As the new replaces the old
And the wheel of the seasons goes on.
Ever the same, ever changing.
Hear us O great Goddess, my sister!
Grant us your favors
Of joy, of love, of peace
And give them to a world
That needs your blessings so deeply.
Blessed Be!

ALL: Blessed Be!

She places the candle holder in the hands of the
mother-priestess, saying:

As the Mother of All
Does hold the lights of the worlds
So also, mother, will you hold this?

The priest brings wine and the loaf or pork. The maiden-priestess holds her hands out over them in blessing and says:

Bless and charge this food
As an offering to you, O Goddess,
That as we partake of it
So we will be strengthened
In your love
And enter the new season
With joy.
Blessed Be!

ALL: **Blessed Be!**

All do eat, and drink. The rite is then opened to any others who wish to add to it. When all is finally ended the ritual is closed by the mother-priestess as she puts out the candles and the tree lights, then proclaims the ceremony to be ended.

III: LADY DAY
(February Eve)

For this rite the altar should be placed at the center of the ritual area and covered with straw matting, but otherwise arranged as usual. Two candles should be placed on the altar, and thirteen initially placed before it, to be lit during the ritual. A crystal or glass ball should be placed on the altar before the Goddess image.

When all is in readiness the priestess shall light each of the thirteen candles, giving each to a person taking part in the rite, to be placed evenly along the edge of the ritual area. She then shall light the incense and the candles on the altar, saying:

> O Goddess of Fire
> Place your warmth about us,
> We do ask.

The priest then says:

> The place of this ritual
> Is now consecrated to the honor
> Of the Old Ones.
> This is a time that is not a time
> In a place that is not a place
> On a day that is not a day
> Between the worlds
> And beyond . . .

After a pause of five heartbeats the priestess says:

> We in our souls, and each in his house
> Must prepare a place for the Lady.
> Let us look within the crystal
> For this, and for other lore
> Which the elemental powers
> Would have us know.

All do link hands and look within for a while. When the priestess (or another skilled in scrying) thinks it appropriate, she shall tell all to rest, and ask what each has had in the way of impressions, what sights may have been seen, what words "heard." If she sees fit, then this part of the rite may be repeated. Afterwards, the ritual should be opened to any who so desire, for singing, for poetry, for teaching, or for meditation exercises. To close the rite the priest directs those in the ceremony to put out the candles which they had placed at the start. He then extinguishes the candles on the altar and proclaims the rite to be ended.

IV. THE FESTIVAL OF THE TREES
(Spring Equinox)

Each person attending the ritual should bring a few leaves or twigs from three or more trees, and a handful of fresh, living tree seeds. Each coming to the rite should also bring food and drink for the feast which follows this ceremony. If at all possible, this ritual should be held in a forest, near an open area which needs new trees. A cauldron or similar vessel shall be placed or hung at the center of the ritual area, and a few small logs of hickory or pine placed beneath it. The cauldron should be filled half full of water, some saltpeter added, and the logs set aflame. It should burn for a while before the ritual begins.

    Those in the ritual shall gather about the flame and cauldron, and look within the flames. When the priestess feels that it is time to begin, she shall stand to the west of the cauldron, facing east. Holding her hands out before her she invokes:

> O Goddess of the Earth,
> Be among us now in your aspect
> As Maiden of the Forest.
> The fair one who brings
> Joy and new life . . .
> To break the winters' stillness
> And silence.

30

The priest shall take her place and, standing as did she, call:

> O laughing God of the Greenwood,
> With your pipes and cloven hooves,
> Shepherd of creatures free and
>   wild,
> Join us here, and with your warmth,
> Let life be born anew.

The priestess throws a handful of odiferous herbs (possibly including ivy, camomile, mint, rose petals and others) into the cauldron, saying:

> Friends, let us all place
> In this cauldron
> The tokens which we have
> Brought to this place.

Going clockwise about the cauldron, each shall throw her, or his, leaves or twigs into the cauldron, saying:

> May the strength of the old
> Enter into the new,
> And life arise once more.

If there is music it should be started at this time, for when all are done the priestess and priest shall lead in a procession clockwise about the cauldron, slowly at first, then faster and yet faster, breaking into a fast dance and continuing. When the priestess and priest feel that the dance is done they shall call all to a halt and to a rest. The priestess or priest shall invoke over the cauldron:

O Great Ones of the forest,
Make this potion strong
And giving of new life.
Blessed Be!

ALL: **Blessed Be!**

Taking some of the cooled potion, all should go forth in different directions to plant their seeds. Men and women should be paired, if possible. Men alone or women alone should offer a brief invocation to the Maiden or to the Horned one as the seeds are planted and watered. When women and men are paired they should work together in planting, and exchange a kiss or other mark of affection as each seed is placed and watered with the potion.

When the planting is done, all should return to the ritual place for dancing, food, drink, and teaching or meditation as desired.

Whatever remains of the potion may be divided among the celebrants and kept for the watering of flowers, trees, or other growing plants.

V. BELTANE
(May Day)

All at the place of ritual should dress brightly and gaily; all should wear flowers and greenery in their hair and clothes. A pole about eight feet high is raised, decorated by everyone prior to the rite with ribbons, greenery, and flowers. It may also be circled with thirteen candles or torches. A wreath or archway of branches and leaves (preferably birch), large enough to step through, should be fashioned near the Beltane Pole . . . from the living branches of a tree, if possible. A glass ball or "black mirror" should be wreathed in leaves and flowers and placed nearby. Several cups of herbal incense may be placed about the ritual area and lit. All at the ritual should bring along refreshments (cakes are traditional) for the feasting afterwards. If the rite is done outdoors all should carry torches. If indoors, candles should be held. The altar should be set to the east and arranged as usual. Five candles should be placed on or about it. As all do stand facing east (women with men if possible) the woman chosen to be priestess shall take the wand in her hands and, holding it over her in salute, shall say:

> Friends, light the brands you hold.
> For here we celebrate
> The sacred night of Beltane
> And the flowering-forth
> Of the woods and meadows.

The man chosen to be the priest then takes the wand similarly and says:

> We here do call and bid
> Our Goddess to be with us.
> She once called "The Lady of May."
> The Goddess of things wild
> Of trees, of skies, and of waters.
> Be with us here.
> Blessed Be!

ALL: **Blessed Be!**

The priestess may take the wand and place it in her sash or belt, or near the pole. The priest, or one chosen by him, shall place a crown of flowers on the head of the priestess. Then the priestess, or one chosen by her, shall place a mask or garland of leaves on the head of the priest. The priestess and priest lead the others into a circle about the Beltane Pole; the procession circles it once clockwise, then all place their candles or torches to the outside. All should stand in a circle about the pole, linked by hands (man to woman, if possible) or hands about each others' waists. All should begin moving sunwise (clockwise) as the priestess slowly chants:

> Here we gather once again.
> Let the sleeper wake.
> May the old ones now return.
> Let the sleeper wake.
> Once again let earth and sky be
>   clean.
> Let the sleeper wake.
> Once more let stream and field be
>   pure.
> Let the sleeper wake.
> Forests spreading, peace returning . . .
>
> Let the sleeper wake.
> May the Lady's touch touch touch be
> On the land once more
> Let the sleeper wake.
> Blessed Be!

ALL: **Blessed Be, Blessed Be, Blessed Be, etc.**

This should continue until nine turns are made about the pole, then all halt. The priestess takes the wand and points at the Beltane Pole, saying to all:

> All of you, friends, look upon the pole
> Seeing in your minds' eyes the pure
>   life force
> Rising through it from the earth,
> Blossoming overhead,
> And cascading down through us
> Flowing out from us to the Lady's
>   world beyond . . .
> Look . . . and see life!

34

She should let all remain for the space of about 25 heartbeats, or possibly longer, as she sees fit.

Then the mirror or crystal is brought forth, wreathed in its garland. The priestess or priest directs each, in turn, to look within it and tell what feeling, impression, or picture comes. All may discuss it as they do rest.

Afterwards, there may be used other forms of divination. Feasting and dancing are in order for as long as all do desire.

VI. MIDSUMMER DAY

This rite should, if at all possible, be done out of doors and on a hilltop. Well before the ritual, all should pile up the materials for a bonfire. Traditionally a wheel is wrapped in branches or straw and either placed atop or next to the bonfire-pile. (If indoors, many candles should be arranged on and about a wooden wheel at the center of the ritual area.) Games and contests of all sorts ... done entirely for fun ... are in order before the rite. A large ring of stones should be made about the bonfire area. The tree nearest the bonfire may be decorated with ribbons before the rite, or a bush may be so bedecked after having been transplanted into the southern part of the circle. (If indoors, a potted flowering bush may be so placed.) Brandy, cakes, and other refreshments should be placed at the base of the tree.

The priestess remains at the ritual area, quietly communing with the Goddess, while the priest gathers the rest together. He has them decorate their clothes with sprays of leaves, the women weaving and wearing garlands if they like. When all are ready the women shall take up knives or shears, and each join her man. All take up torches (or candles, if indoors) which the priest lights, saying:

The fire festival has begun.
Let us go forth
And celebrate

35

This golden season.
In the names of the Old Ones.
Blessed Be!

ALL: **Blessed Be!**

He leads them on a roundabout procession, carrying their brands, to the place of the rite. As they approach the circle of stone the priestess halts them and challenges:

PRIESTESS: **Who comes here . . .**
To this place held sacred
To the Old Gods?

PRIEST: **I come, my lady.**
Leading others who would
Do honor to the Great Ones.

PRIESTESS: **Then I, as the one who**
Stands here for the Goddess,
Do bid you welcome.
Enter, and light the fire.

All enter the circle and throw their torches on the bonfire pile. (If indoors, all light the wheel-candles and place their candles at the center. As the fire grows, all do look within the flames as the priestess spreads her arms and invokes:

Green Forest Mother
Be with us here in
Your fullness of limb
We do ask.
Blessed Be!

ALL: **Blessed Be!**

What follows next is especially done in a spirit of joking and good humor. The priestess says to all:

> Friends, at this, the Night of Mid-
> summer
> Does the Goddess reign supreme.
> At this time does she have power
> Over her horned consort.
> And in commemoration of this I bid
> you . . .
>
> Go to your man, and cut
> A bit of his hair . . . as much as you do
> like . . .
> And throw it in the Lady's fire.
> In honor of Her!
> Go!

If there are extra men or extra women, they should encourage and advise those who do the cutting. As the last couple is done, throw the hair into the fire (if indoors burn the bits of hair with incense in a brazier) the priest has music started, and all dance sunwise (clockwise) about the circle. The music should be fast and spirited, and dancing humorous, spontaneous and enjoyable, until all are ready to rest. All may relax before the tree and about the fire as the priest holds his hands out over the food and drink, saying:

> Blessed Lady of the Forest
> And friends of the wilds,
> Place your blessing on this food and
> drink,
> That it may strengthen us in your
> ways

Of joy and mystery.
Blessed Be!

ALL: **Blessed Be!**

The refreshments may be passed out at this time.More dancing, music and singing are in order, for as long as is desired, and others may add to the rite as they see fit. When it is desired to end the ritual, the priestess shall stand before the fire and say:

Remove the stones and break the
    circle.
Our revelry is done, friends.
Those whom we cannot see
We do thank for being here.
The rite is ended!
Blessed Be!

ALL: **Blessed Be!**

☆ ☆ ☆

VII.   AUGUST EVE
(Lammas)

The place of this rite should have sheaves of grain placed at each of the four quarters just outside the ritual area. At the center should be a cauldron large enough for the flame desired, filled mostly with water but with about an inch of vegetable oil added, and a floating wick if necessary. Some perfumed oils may be added for a scent. Thirteen candles are initially placed about the cauldron, to be lit during the ritual. If possible, someone should fashion a small cat, hare, or dog from straw, placing it next to the cauldron on the western side.

When all is in readiness the priest shall light each of the thirteen candles, giving each to one person within the circle, to be placed evenly along the edge of the ritual area, more or less in the form of a circle. The priestess shall then set a flame in the cauldron, and standing before it with her arms outstretched shall say:

> O ancient ones of days long past,
> We do ask your presence
> Here among us.
> For this is a time that is not a time
> In a place that is not a place
> On a day that is not a day
> Between the worlds
> And beyond . . .

She raps three times on the cauldron. After a pause of five heartbeats the priest says:

> The harvest season draws forth,
> For this is the height of the year.
> The bounty of this rich season
> Shall sustain us
> In seasons to come
> In spirit, in soul, in body.

A processional spiral is led by the priestess five times about the cauldron. Then music is started and there is informal dancing which should move generally clockwise about the cauldron. When it is appropriate all shall rest while the priestess or priest explains some of the significance of this festival. Afterwards, the rite should be opened to any who so desire, for singing, for poetry, for scrying, or for teaching. More dancing may follow, if it is desired. To close the rite the priestess orders those in the ceremony to put out the candles which they had placed at the start. She then proclaims the ritual to be ended.

☆ ☆ ☆

VIII.   FALL EQUINOX

Many fruits, vegetables, and other natural foods are to be placed about the altar, as are wine and glasses for all present. The altar itself is set up as usual, though scattered with autumn leaves. An elder woman should be chosen to act as the priestess, for this is the season of the Crone.

To begin, the priestess lights the three candles upon the altar as the rest gather about. She says:

> In the Name of the Goddess
> And under Her protection
> Is this rite now begun.

The priestess and the priest face each other from opposite sides of the altar. The priest says:

> The crane flies south
> And winter must come.
> The green seasons are past
> And winds shall be cold . . .

PRIESTESS: So now we must prepare
Without and within,
For the hard seasons
Which lie before us.

PRIEST: As we shall store up food for the body,
So also must we put in store
Strength for the spirit,
Until the spring is born again.

The priestess spreads wide her arms and invokes:

> We do ask, O Goddess wise,
> That your blessings may surround
> us.
> And we thank you for this plentiful
> food
> Which you have given us.
> Cast your blessing upon this bounty,
> That it may especially strengthen us
> And lead us in your hidden ways.
> Blessed Be!

ALL: **Blessed Be!**

The priest opens the wine and pours for all. As all do hold forth their glasses he announces:

PRIEST: Friends, I proclaim a toast.
To the good seasons which have
gone,
And the good ones yet to come.

ALL: **Blessed Be!**

PRIEST: Friends, I proclaim a toast.
To the beauty of autumn
And to the good friends we treasure.

ALL: **Blessed Be!**

PRIEST: Friends, I proclaim a toast.
To the Goddess!
May She bring peace back to the
world!

ALL: **Blessed Be!**

41

Meditation exercises may be done, and the rite may at this time be opened to any in the group who wishes to add to the above. Singing and the playing of musical instruments are also appropriate.

To close the ritual the priestess puts out the candles and proclaims that the rite is done.

After the rite some of the foodstuffs which have been blessed during the ceremony should be prepared and cured, preserved, or canned by those who took part in the rite. These foods may be used in later seasonal rituals.

Marriage Rite

This rite is best performed at the time of the new moon. The place of the marriage rite should be decked with flowers of many kinds. The altar should be placed at the eastern edge of the ritual area, and arranged as usual, with a willow wand and two white candles. Incense should be of a flower scent such as apple, rose, cherry blossom, or such. The couple to be wedded may dress as they desire, though it is an ancient Celtic custom that the bride wear a veil or net, and an article of red or scarlet. The couple should each obtain and wrap a small symbolic gift for the other; these gifts should be placed on the altar before the start of the ceremony. Wine and a cake or cakes should be provided for the revel to follow. The wedding rings should be given to the priest just before the ritual. He will fit them over the wand and replace them on the altar.

To begin, the priestess and priest light the candles and incense. They turn toward the others in the rite, the priestess to the right of the priest and their backs to the altar. The priest holds his right hand aloft and says:

> May the place of this rite
> Be consecrated before the gods.
> For we gather here in a ritual of love
> With two who would be wedded.
> ———— and ———— come
> forward
> And stand here before us
> And before the gods of nature.

The two to be wedded come forward at this time, the man to the right of the woman, and stop before the priestess and priest. The priestess says:

43

Be with us here, O beings of the air.
With your clever fingers
Tie closely the bonds between these
two.
Be with us here, O beings of fire.
Give their love and passion
Your own all-consuming ardor.
Be with us here, O beings of water.
Give them the deepest of love
And richness of body, of soul, and of
spirit.
Be with us here, O beings of earth.
Let your strength and constancy
Be theirs for so long as they desire
To remain together.
Blessed Goddess and Laughing God
Give to these before us, we do ask,
Your love and protection.
Blessed Be!

ALL: **Blessed Be!**

The priest picks up the wand and rings and holds one end of it before him in his right hand, the priestess likewise holds the other end with her left hand, the rings on the exposed wand between them. The priestess then says to the two before her:

Place your right hands
Over this wand, and your rings.
His hand over hers.

The priest then says:

Above you are the stars
Below you the stones.
As time does pass
Remember ...
Like a star should your love be
constant.
Like a stone should your love be firm.
Be close, yet not too close.
Possess one another, yet be
understanding.
Have patience each with the other
For storms will come, but they will go
quickly.
Be free in giving of affection and
warmth
Make love often, and be sensuous to
one another.
Have no fear, and let not the ways or
words
Of the unenlightened give you
unease.
For the Goddess and the God are
with you.
Now and always.

After a pause of five heartbeats the priestess says:

Is it your wish (bride's name) to
become one
With this man?
(The answer is given by the
bride)
Is it your wish (groom's name) to
become one

With this woman?
> (The answer is given by the
> groom)

Do any say nay?

Then as the Goddess, the God, and
> the Old Ones

Are witness to this rite

I now proclaim you husband and
> wife!

A kiss is appropriate at this time. When the gifts have been opened the ritual is considered to be ended.

The Going of the Ways

Not every couple will desire to stay wedded, for each person is an individual and some will differ too much to remain together. The decision to part is not one to be undertaken lightly ... but if all else fails then this final rite is to be performed.

The couple to be parted will spend as much time as necessary with the priestess and priest to agree on a fair division of property between the two, and provisions for support of children, if there are any. These and any other items of importance must be committed to paper and witnessed by the priestess and priest. The priest should arrange to have this document notarized, and copies prepared for each.

The altar should be placed at the western edge of the ritual area, and arranged as usual with two candles. A sharp double-edged knife should be placed before the image of the lady, and a picture of the two who will be parting. To begin, the priestess and priest light the candles and incense. They turn toward the others in the rite, the priestess to the right of the priest and their backs to the altar. The priest holds his right hand aloft and says:

> May the place of this rite
> Be consecrated before the Old Ones.
> For we gather here to perform
> That which must be done.
> _____ and _____ , come forward
> And stand here before us.

The two come forward at this time, the man to the right of the woman, and stop before the priestess and priest. The priestess says:

You both fully know
The import of this step.
So now for the very last time . . .
Do you wish, _____ , to part?
    (The woman answers.)
Do you wish, _____ , to part?
    (The man answers.)

If one or both say "no," then the rite will be halted and an attempt at reconciliation made. If this attempt fails, or if both say "yes," the priestess will take the picture from the altar, place it in the incense smoke for a moment, and give it to the couple before her, saying:

Here in this place
And before the eys of the Old Ones
And the creatures of the elements
I bid you to destroy
This symbol of your life together.

The two will tear and shred the picture, and give the pieces to the priest. He shall place the pieces in the incense brazier and set them afire, while the priestess ties a light cord about the right wrist of both the woman and the man, leaving a hand's-length of cord between them. The priest takes the knife from the altar and holds it aloft in salute as he stands before the woman and man. He invokes:

We do ask you, O Blessed Lady
And most revered God
To heal the wounds of parting
And to comfort the hearts
Of those who do feel pain.
When both have gone their ways
Let love, and not bitterness, remain
    within.

He quickly cuts the cord which binds their wrists, saying:

> You are free.

The priestess says:

> Go now, and go in peace.
> For this rite
> Is ended.

The priest will file whatever paperwork is required to make the separation final.

(If one of the couple is not available and all do agree that the parting of the ways is necessary, then a priest or priestess of another group will take the place of the missing partner for this ritual.)

Rite for the Dead

If one has lost a member of his or her family and desires a Pagan ceremony at the interment, this rite may be performed.

As the coffin is carried to the burying-ground, four torchbearers should accompany it — one before the pall-bearers, one behind, and one on either side. The priestess and priest shall walk at the head of the procession of mourners. The nearest of kin should walk with them. The priestess should carry three boughs of evergreen, and flowers; others in the procession should be encouraged to carry flowers also. The priest should have placed a net over the coffin.

As the coffin is placed in the grave the priest shall place one torch-bearer at the foot of the grave, one at either side, and one behind the priest, priestess and family who all do stand at the head. When all is in readiness, the priest will hold both hands aloft and say:

> We gather here now
> To bid farewell to a friend
> Who must travel far.
> The blessings of the Goddess,
> Of the God, of the Old Ones
> And of good friends
> Are with you
> As you travel beyond.

If it is so desired by friends and family, the priestess or priest, or others, may at this time give a brief eulogy for the departed. If singing is desired it, too, should be done at this time. The priest shall say, then:

There is a reason for being here
In this world and this life.
There is a reason for leaving,
When the purposes of this life are
     done.
The soul must journey beyond
To pause, to rest,
To wait for those who are loved.

For the world beyond is a land
Of eternal summer, and of joy,
Far from the cares of this world,
With happiness and with youth
     anew.

There is a pause for a few moments.
The priestess shall place the three boughs of evergreen
atop the coffin, saying:

As the evergreen does grow and
     prosper
Both in summer and in winter, year
     after year,
So also does the soul continue
From life to life to life . . .
Growing ever stronger, wiser, and
     richer.

The priest then places flowers upon the casket, saying:

May the servants of the gods
Escort you with honor
To their own land

**Of light, of beauty, and of joy.
Blessed Be!**

ALL: **Blessed Be!**

Flowers should be strewn on and about the coffin by all present. All those who are present should retire to relax, and have a memorial dinner. All should endeavor to by degrees turn sorrow into lightheartedness and joy, for with death only the physical body is lost . . . and nothing more.

The four torches should be stuck in the ground about the grave and left there to burn out.

The Solitary Rituals

I. SELF BLESSING

This ritual should be performed during the new moon, but it is not limited to that phase. Need, not season, determines the performance. There is real power in the Self Blessing; it should not be used other than in time of need and should not be done promiscuously.

The purpose of the ritual is to bring the individual into closer contact with the Godhead. It can also be used as a minor dedication, when a person who desires dedication has no one who can dedicate him. This self blessing ritual may also be used as a minor exorcism, to banish any evil influences which may have formed around the person. It may be performed by any person upon himself, and at his desire.

Perform the ritual in a quiet place, free from distractions, and nude. You will need the following:

1. Salt, about one quarter teaspoon.
2. Wine, about an ounce.
3. Water, about one-half ounce.
4. Candle, votive or other.

The result of the ritual is a feeling of peace and calm. It is desirable that the participant bask in the afterglow so that he may meditate and understand that he has called the attention of the Godhead to himself, asking to grow closer to the Godhead in both goals and in wisdom.

When you are ready to begin, sprinkle the salt on the floor and stand on it, lighting the candle. Let the warmth of the candle be absorbed into the body. Mix the water into the wine, meditating upon your reasons for performing the self blessing.

Read the following aloud:

Bless me, Mother, for I am Thy child.

Dip the fingers of the right hand into the mixed water and wine and anoint the eyes,

> Blessed be my eyes, that I may see Thy path.

Anoint the nose,

> Blessed be my nose, that I may breathe Thy essence.

Anoint the mouth,

> Blessed be my mouth, that I may speak of Thee.

Anoint the breast,

> Blessed be my breast, that I may be faithful in Thy works.

Anoint the loins,

> Blessed be my loins, which bring forth the life of man as Thou has brought forth all creation.

Anoint the feet,

> Blessed be my feet, that I may walk in Thy ways.

Remain . . . and meditate for a while.

II. SOLITARY RITUAL FOR THE FULL MOON

If no others of like interest are available at the time of the full moon, the following rite may be accomplished by a solitary individual.

The ritual should be performed at the time of the full moon and preferably near midnight. It should be accomplished out-of-doors or, failing that, at a window through which the moonlight may shine upon the worshipper.

The robe or gown or other apparel worn for this ceremony should be unique and "magical" or "witchy" in its cut and feel. It should, if possible, be worn only for ritual and magical purposes. (Essentially, however, any garb ... or none at all ... may be worn.) Before dressing for the ceremony one should bathe, bearing strongly in the mind that the water is "cleansing the soul and spirit," as well as the body.

Go alone to a place of solitude which you have selected previously, or to the room which you have prepared, carrying with you the implements needed for the rite.

Build at the spot a circle of 13 stones, each being about the size of a man's head, for the outdoor rite. If the ritual is to be held indoors smaller stones may be used. Lay the stones down starting from the north and working clockwise about the eight-foot circle. Two additional stones should be placed at the center to support a small, simple altar ... or to serve as an altar in themselves. One altar-stone should be to the east of the circle's centerpoint and the other placed next to it at the west of the centerpoint.

Place an image of the Goddess on the altar, and light incense before it. A cup or goblet of wine about half full should be placed before the image of the Lady. A copy of this ritual may also be placed where it can be easily seen.

If the ritual is held out-of-doors, torches should be used if no other persons are about. Indoors, white or blue candles may be used. A candle or torch should be placed at each side of the altar, as you say:

> My Lady of silver magic.
> I do build this circle ...
> A place sacred and apart ...
> In your honor.

Place a light at the North point of the circle, saying:

> Blessed One, the earth is yours.
> May it become fertile and rich
> And free from spoil.

Place a light at the East point of the circle, saying:

> O Lady of laughter and cheer,
> The skies are yours.
> May the air be clear and sweet
> And the clouds giving of soft rains.

Place a light at the South point of the circle, saying:

> O Goddess of warmth,
> The seasons are yours.
> May each spring bring forth
> More richness of the natural world.

Place a light at the West point of the circle, saying:

> Lovely One, the sparkling waters are
>   yours.
> May the streams and rivers
> Flow pure and clear
> Once more.

Stand before the altar and image of the Lady . . . in view of the moon, if possible . . . and raise your arms out toward the moon in salute, invoking in these or similar words:

My Lady of silver magic.
I have built this sacred place
For you, and in your honor.
I do ask that your gracious presence
Be with me here.

Stand silently for a while, with arms out and eyes closed, meditating on the presence of a mysterious and magical Goddess . . . She who was greeted and known by your own distant ancestors, in rites much like this, in times long past. Meditate on Her being present once again. And close at hand.

Kneel before the altar, facing the image of the Lady, and take up the goblet of wine, saying:

In honor of you, my Lady,
Do I pour this libation
And drink this toast.

Pour a few drops out before the altar, and drink. Now is the time to sit and relax. Meditation on the Goddess in Her many aspects is in order, as are various types of divination. Folk songs of love and magic may be sung, if this is your inclination, or poetry read.

When you feel that the rite should end, put out the torches or candles at the north, east, south, and west in that order. Kneel at the altar, saying:

O gracious and lovely one,
I thank you for strengthening me
With your presence.
May all magic and power be yours!
Blessed Be!

Put out the torches or candles by the altar. Then state:

The rite is ended.

☆ ☆ ☆

III. SOLITARY RITUAL FOR SAMHAIN

As benefits this festival, you should dress in a particularly striking and "magical" manner. Jewelry, ornaments, and ritual instruments you have used in previous rites or which you feel are of particular personal value to you should be used in this rite. This is the one ritual in which you may, if such is your taste, wear a dagger, sword, or other weapon: the purpose is to emphasize the power that you, the Pagan, have over those forces that are not of this world. Such power is at its best when it is available, but not flaunted.

The altar should be set as usual, but with three candles placed on it. Five candles of varying, seasonal colors, should be placed before the altar, to be lit later. A pentagram should be marked on the ritual area, centered on the spot where you will be sitting before the altar. The pentacle should be about eight feet across. It would be appropriate to place a pumpkin and some ears of corn to one side of the altar and a small cauldron (or suitable substitute) to the other side. On the altar place a bit of bread and some salt in a small dish, as well as a glass or goblet containing some red wine. Much incense should be available, and used liberally throughout the ceremony.

Set up the ritual area in advance, then retire to bathe before robing for this rite, fixing in your mind that the water is cleansing not just the physical body, but also the heart, spirit, and soul of all guilt, stain and imperfection . . . leaving behind only that which is strong and good.

When you are prepared, meditate for a while. Consider that in ancient times this night marked the end of the year, and that on this evening the veil between the worlds was thin. And that this was a night of warmth, welcome, and good cheer toward family, friends and for those who had passed beyond.

Go alone to the place of the ritual, and kneel before the altar. Light the candles on the altar, saying as you do so:

Light candle.

> This I light for the Maiden's bright
>   glory.

Light candle.

> This I light for the passion and
>   triumph of the Lady.

Light candle.

> This for the wisdom of the Crone.

Light the incense, and then the five candles which sit before the altar, saying:

> These do I light in honor
> Not only of the Three-Fold Goddess
> But for Her strong, horned consort.
> He who is sometimes laughing,
>   sometimes grim
> And close nearby on this night.

Stand, pointing the wand out before you, calling:

> On this, the sacred night of Samhain
> Do I build this small temple
> In honor of the Goddess, and of the
>   God
> And of the Ancient Ones
> From the times before Time.
> To all I do give my love
> And my warmest greetings.

Place the five candles at the points of the pentagram, touching each with the wand. Rap thrice upon the altar with the wand, then replace it. Kneel before the altar and hold your arms out over it, crossed, and give the incantation:

> This is a time that is not a time
> In a place that is not a place
> On a day that is not a day
> Between the worlds
> And beyond . . .

Pause for the space of 13 heartbeats. Then hold your hands over the bread, the salt, and the wine in an attitude of blessing, and say:

> For this salt, bread, and wine
> Do I ask the blessings
> Of Maiden, of Lady, of Crone
> And of the Horned One
> Who guards the Portal of the Worlds

Take the bread and touch it to the salt, saying:

> May I, and those whom I love
> Have sufficiency and good health.

After eating the bread, take the wine cup and hold it forth in a toast toward the north, saying:

> May our spirits be strong.

Drink the wine, and proclaim:

By the Threefold Goddess
And by the Horned God
So be it!

At this time you may relax, play a musical instrument, and sing or recite poetry, if these are your inclinations. Or you may improvise that which you feel is appropriate for this occasion. Song or rhyme may concern death, the supernatural and times far past, but they should also include love, joy, and good fellowship. If a source of music is available you may want to improvise a solitary "Dance of Hallowe'en" or suitable procession clockwise about the ritual area. When you feel that the ritual should end, put out the candles at the points of the pentacle, then those of the altar, saying:

Though these flames
Of the material world
Be darkened,
They shall ever burn
In the worlds beyond.
The rite is ended!

IV. SOLITARY RITUAL FOR YULE

This rite should be performed late on the Eve of Yule, December 24. The robe, gown, or other apparel worn for this ceremony should be unique and "magical" in its cut and feel, if at all possible. The jewelry and ornamentation worn at this time should ideally reflect the season's decor.

The most ancient of pagan traditions, the Yule Tree, is used in this rite. The tree, fully trimmed and decorated (in a suitably Pagan manner), should be placed five to eight feet to the east of the altar. The altar is set as usual, though facing toward the tree; two colored, seasonal candles are placed on the altar. Many decorations and colored lights should be placed about the ritual area: these are to be lit once the ritual has begun. A small bit of incense . . . frankincense, if it is available . . . should be wrapped as a gift of the season and placed before the altar. Some food (pork or turkey, preferably) and wine should be set next to the altar.

Set up the ritual area in advance, then retire to bathe before dressing for this rite, fixing in your mind that the water is cleansing not just the physical body, but your very soul of all guilt, stain, and imperfection, leaving that which is strong, good, and richly alive.

When all is in readiness and you are prepared, go to the darkened ritual area and sit near the altar. Meditate for a while that this, to our ancient ancestors, was the "low part" of the year. The harvest was long past, the days were cold and short. It was, in essence, the Season of Death . . . for all things must die. Yet new life must spring from death, as life becomes incarnate once more. And this festival was the time of first rebirth. Light one candle, and then the other, saying:

> **The darkness of the season**
> **Shall be broken**
> **And new life be born**
> **Once again.**

Take the two candles, one in each hand, and go to the south side of the darkened room, and hold them out in salute to the Pagan deities. Repeat this to the west, the north, and finally to the east. Replace the candles on the altar and say:

> **In this, the Season of the White**
> **Goddess**
> **Do I celebrate the festival of Yule,**
> **The rebirth of the sun,**
> **And of life for the coming year.**
> **This eternal cycle**
> **Do I mark here.**

Fire up all the decorative lights at this time, and return to your place before the altar. Sit and meditate briefly. Hold your arms out over the altar, crossed, and say:

> I do give greeting to the God of the
>   Forests
> Who does rule in this season.
> I do give greeting to the lovely
>   Goddess
> By whose blessings and grace
> Shall life always be born again.

Take the wrapped incense package in both hands and stand, holding it up before you:

> This symbolic gift
> I dedicate to you,
> O Ancient Ones!

Pause thus for the space of thirteen heartbeats, then sit, unwrap the package, and light the incense, placing it in a brazier or bowl on the altar.

You may at this point add other parts to the rite as you feel are appropriate: singing or playing of seasonal music (preferably that having more Pagan overtones), reading of poetry, meditation exercises, and the like. If such is your inclination, and if suitable recorded music is available, you may want to improvise your own "Dance of Rebirth," or an appropriate procession about the ritual area.

At a convenient time you should partake of the food and wine. Place it on the altar and, holding your right hand over it in an attitude of blessing, invoke:

> Bless me, O Lady and God of
>   the Wilds,
> And bless this food,
> Which has been your gift
> To us all.

63

Afterwards you may rest, meditate, or continue your own additions to the rite. When at last you feel the ritual should close, hold your arms out over the altar, crossed, and say:

> Lovely Goddess and Laughing God,
> I do thank you for being,
>   in spirit,
> Here with me.
> Blessed Be!

Put out the candles, saying:

> The rite is ended.

Let the decorative lights burn for the rest of the evening, if this is practical.

V. SOLITARY RITUAL FOR LADY DAY

The robe, gown, or other apparel worn for this ceremony should be unique and "witchy" in its cut and feel, if at all possible. Dark colors are appropriate, as is the wearing of much silver (or silver-colored) jewelry.

The altar is set as usual, with two candles upon it. A small sheaf of grain should be placed to the east of the altar and thirteen candles placed about the ritual area itself. A cup of wine is placed on the altar before the image of the Lady.

Set up the ritual area beforehand, then retire (taking one candle from the place of ritual) to bathe before dressing for the rite. As you do so, picture in your mind that the water is cleansing the soul and spirit just as it is cleansing your physical body.

When you have dressed for the rite, sit quietly in a dim place for a while and light the candle. While you are watching it, meditate that in ancient times the Goddess, in Her fiery aspect, was welcomed back to the homes, the temples, and to the land itself in joyous celebrations on this night. Take the candle and walk slowly to the place of the ritual. Sit briefly before the altar, then light the candles and the incense on the altar, invoking:

> **O Goddess of Fire**
> **Place your warmth about me**
> **I do ask.**

Go clockwise about the ritual area, starting at the north, and light all the candles remaining. Then kneel before the altar; take the wand with your right hand and rap thrice, slowly, upon the altar, saying:

> **I give love and greetings**
> **To the blessed Lady**
> **And to Her consort,**
> **The Horned One of death and of life.**

Replace the wand and take the wine-cup in your hands. Holding it up before you, give the toast:

> **I drink, O Ancient Ones**
> **In your honor . . .**
> **And to the coming seasons**
> **Of warmth and of love.**

Drink of the wine, and replace the cup. Pick up a copy of this rite and, walking slowly clockwise about the altar, read the following:

The Lady is come
And we welcome Her.
The creatures of the wilds
Do know She is near
For the world shall soon feel life.
The season is harsh;
The Horned God rules
At this bitter time . . .
And this is fore-ordained.
But She does return
And life shall soon come
To forest, field, and glen.

Stop before the altar, saying:

Blessed Be!

At this time you may perform meditation exercises, read or recite poetry about the return of life after the winter, or do else which is appropriate for this night. If a source of music is available a solitary "Dance of the Lady's Return" may be improvised, if this is your inclination.

To close the ritual, kneel before the altar and spread out your arms, calling:

I do ask, O Goddess and God of the
    ancient ways,
That your blessings may be spread
    wide.
So that the world may be led back
To your ways of peace and joy.
Blessed Be!

Put out all candles but those on the altar. As you blow out these last two, say:

The rite is ended.

VI. SOLITARY FESTIVAL OF THE TREES

The robe, gown, or other clothing worn for this ceremony should be striking and "magical" in appearance. Some leaves and flowers should be worn on your clothes or in your hair, according to taste.

You should bring a few leaves or twigs from three or more trees, and a handful of fresh tree seeds or nuts. If at all possible, this ritual should be held in a forest, near an open area which needs new trees. If conditions dictate that the rite be held indoors, plan an outing to such a forested area to follow very soon after the ritual . . . immediately, if possible.

A cauldron or similar vessel should be placed or hung at the center of the ritual area. Fill it part way with fresh water, and add a little saltpeter; set a fire beneath it. If you have brought along some food and drink, place those items nearby.

Stand to the west of the cauldron, facing east, when you feel that the rite should begin. Hold the wand out in your right hand over the cauldron and invoke:

> **O Goddess of the Earth,**
> **Be with me now in your aspect**
> **As Maiden of the forest . . .**
> **The fair one who brings**
> **Joy and new life . . .**
> **To break the winter's stillness**
> **And silence.**

Rap once upon the cauldron with the wand.

> **O laughing God of the Greenwood**
> **With your pipes and cloven hooves,**
> **Shepherd of creatures free and wild,**
> **Come nearby, and with your warmth**
> **Let life be born anew.**

Rap once upon the cauldron with the wand. Then drop in the twigs and leaves you have brought along, one at a time, saying:

> **May the strength of the old**
> **Enter into the new**
> **And life arise once more.**
> **O Great Ones of the forest**
> **Make this potion strong**
> **And giving of new life.**
> **Blessed Be.**

Take the cauldron from off the flame and let it cool. Over the food which you have brought, say a short blessing of thanks to the Goddess, and partake of it. When you have finished and the cauldron has cooled, take some or all of the liquid within and walk to the place which you have chosen to plant the trees. At each place, poke or dig the hole with the wand, pour in some of the potion, and give a brief invocation to the Lady or to the Horned One as you cover it. When you are done, find a clearing within the forest and speak quietly to the Gods, thanking them and asking that the seeds grow swiftly. Then proclaim the ritual to be ended.

VII. SOLITARY BELTANE RITUAL

For this ritual one should dress brightly and strikingly, wearing flowers and greenery according to taste. A low altar should be built partially or entirely of stones at the middle of the ritual area ... this being done by yourself earlier. Two candles should be placed on the altar, and the altar itself arranged as usual. (If the ritual is performed out-of-doors the candles may be replaced by torches. These may be stuck in the ground on either side of the altar.) Four candles or torches are placed before the altar to be lit later. A vertical pole about three feet in height is usually erected on the far side of the altar: it should be decked with fruits, flowers, and bright ribbons. A goblet or cup half full of wine should be placed before the image of the Goddess.

Before dressing for the ceremony, one should bathe, bearing strongly in mind that the water is cleansing not only the body, but even the soul itself.

When you are prepared for the rite, meditate for a while before going into the ritual area, thinking strongly on the old pagan ways and trying to imagine the rituals which took place on this night in ages past.

Go alone to the place of solitude which you have prepared for your rite. Kneeling before the altar, light the candles (or torches) on the altar, and the incense. Set alight the four candles or brands before the altar and place them three or five feet from the altar at the north, east, south and west, saying:

> Here at this spot
> Do I create a place
> Sacred to the gods of old.
> For a while, here and now
> Shall the ancient ways
> Live again.

Take the wand and hold it out in salute toward the East, saying:

O winds of the East
Blow sweet and pure
For the Lady reigns again!

Hold the wand out in salute toward the South, saying:

O warmth of the South
Bring forth life from the earth
For the Lady reigns again!

Hold the wand out in salute toward the West, saying:

O waters of the West
Glisten clear and fresh
For the Lady reigns again!

Hold the wand out in salute toward the North, saying:

O lands of the North
Grow rich and bounteous
For the Lady reigns again!

Then replace the wand and, holding your arms out over the altar, say:

Gracious and lovely Lady of the
    moon,
Of joy and of love,
Protectress of forests and wild
    things,
This place is consecrated to thee.

Take up the wine cup, hold it out at arm's length, and pour out a few drops, saying:

To the great ones of old
And to the joyous times to come!

Drink some. After a brief pause, rap three times on the altar with the wand, saying:

As woods and meadows flower forth
I celebrate the ancient rite
As the ancients did before me.
I cast the words into the mists
Of time and space and otherwhere:
Where one stays now, in years to
    come,
May scores of others revel there.
So may it be!

Rap once upon the altar with the wand. Incense should be added now. Your own additions to the rite are appropriate now: meditations, poetry, songs, divination, and the like. If a source of proper music is available a solitary "Dance of the Winds" may be improvised. When all is done, close by rapping four times with the wand, saying:

Friends of the nether worlds
Who have been about me for a while
You may, with thanks,
Return from whence you came.

Hold arms out and say:

Blessed Lady of joy and laughter
I thank you for your presence.
May some of your love and soft
    power
Remain with me.
Blessed Be!

Put out the lights about the altar. As the two on the altar itself are darkened, say:

The rite is ended.

VIII. SOLITARY RITUAL FOR LAMMAS

The robe, gown, or other apparel worn for this ceremony should be unique and "magical" in its cut and feel, if at all possible. For this rite the wearing of much ornamentation or jewelry is traditional.

For this rite no altar is required. At the center of the ritual area should be set a small cauldron (or equivalent substitute), with an inch or so of alcohol poured into it. Some scented oil may be added. One or three ears of corn may be placed to one side of the cauldron and a bottle of red brandy, with a small cup, glass, or goblet, placed to the other side. Place four ears of corn before the cauldron for use later, and place 13 stones nearby.

Bathe before dressing for the rite, keeping strongly in mind that the water is not only cleansing the body, but also purifying the soul of weakness and guilt and the dross of the world.

When you are prepared, meditate for a while on the great balance of nature . . . that while the fields at this season are harvested of their rich crops, so also must we soon return as much back to the soil. That which is taken from the earth in *any* form must be taken with respect, and an equivalent worth soon returned. This is always as it has been in the past and must be in the future.

Go alone to the place of the rite and kneel briefly before the cauldron, facing south. Put your hands upon it and say:

> At this spot shall I fashion
> My own small temple,
> Sacred to the Goddess
> And to the gods of long ago.

72

Taking the 13 stones which you have previously piled nearby, start from a point south of the cauldron and place them in a circle about it, working clockwise, leaving room enough inside for you to move about, if this is your intention during the ritual. Then kneel again before the cauldron and touch the liquid inside with a finger and place a drop on each of the four ears of corn before the altar, saying:

> A bond shall thus be formed
> Between the central flame
> And the living seed
> Which shall be about me.

Carefully light the cauldron, then place the four ears of corn at the south, west, north, and east points of the stone circle. Sitting before the cauldron, hold your hands out to the flame, saying:

> This place I have made sacred
> To the gracious Lady
> And to those who serve Her.

Pause briefly, then raise your right hand toward the south in salute, saying:

> O ancient ones of days long past
> I do ask your presence
> Nearby.
> For this is a time that is not a time
> In a place that is not a place
> On a day that is not a day.
> And I am here.
> Blessed Be!

Then pour some of the brandy. Hold the glass forth, raised high above the cauldron flame as you toast:

I drink to the glory of the season,
To the ways of mystery, and of magic
Which were known in ages past
And shall be known again
In times to come.

Drink. If you feel that any other toasts are worthy at this time they should also be performed now. So also should other things which you may desire to add to the rite: meditation exercises, reading or reciting poetry or song about the earth and its richness, and the like. If a source of appropriate music is available a solitary "Dance of the Earth" may be improvised, if this is your inclination.

To close the ritual, kneel before the cauldron and spread your arms outwards, saying:

I do ask, O Goddess wise,
That your blessings may be
About all.
So the children of men
May be led back
To your ways of peace and joy.
Blessed Be!

Gather in the ears of corn and the 13 stones, placing them about the cauldron. As the last is placed thereby, state:

The rite is ended.

Let the cauldron burn itself out, if it has not already done so.

IX. SOLITARY MIDSUMMER RITE

For this ritual a man should dress as if for conflict, but a woman should wear raiment which is soft and feminine. And this ceremonial garb should be chosen also for its magical or witch-like feel and cut. The altar should be set as usual with three candles on it. A wooden wheel or representation thereof should be set on the altar, with the Goddess image and one candle placed within its rim. Or a wheel may itself be made part of the altar. Five candles should be placed before the altar, to be lit later. (As with other such rites, if the following is to be performed out-of-doors then torches may be used in lieu of candles.)

Set up the ritual area beforehand. Then retire (taking one candle) to bathe before dressing for the rite, fixing in your mind that the water is cleansing the soul and heart just as it is cleansing the body.

Light the candle and gaze at it. Meditate for a while: all things change ... yet ultimately are the same. This is "the turning of the year" as all years do turn ...

Take the lit candle or torch and walk slowly to the place of the rite. Sit briefly before the altar, then light the candles or torches thereon, and the incense, saying:

> I do bid the unseen forces of nature
> To gather close about me.
> For I do call forth
> The images of times long past.

Light the five brands or candles before the altar and place them in the form of a pentagram, centered on the altar. (These points should be marked out beforehand.) Place the first candle or torch at the north, and the rest in their positions while working in a clockwise manner about the altar.

Standing again before the altar, pick up the wand and point north, east, south and west, saying:

May winds blow cool
The sun shine warm
The waters bright and pure.
May Earth regain her former glory
And the race of man endure.

Rap thrice upon the altar with the wand and, pointing it upward, say:

O blessed Lady of the moonlight
Be with me here, I do ask.
Stand near as I do perform
This rite in your honor.
Blessed Be!

Replace the wand, then hold your arms out over the altar crossed, and say:

At this, the Night of Midsummer
Does the Goddess reign supreme.
At this time does She reign supreme.
In Her name do I now give praise
And call forth into the mists for times
For times to come which are better.
When men can live in peace and in
    calm
And green forests return once more.
Blessed Be!

Sit, and add incense. Meditate for a while on the season's words: "The sacred king doth yield the power to his dark brother, but the Goddess who loves them reigns ever unchanging."

At this time you may add as you see fit to the ritual: meditation exercises, reading or reciting poetry of love and of nature, or do else which is appropriate for this night. If a source of music is available a solitary "Dance of Power" may be improvised, if this is your inclination.

To close the ritual, rap slowly five times with the wand, saying:

> The hour is done
> The spells are cast
> And honor given
> To the Great Ones
> Of times far past.
> I give love, farewell,
> And blessings
> To the Goddess
> And the Ancients.
> Blessed Be!

Put out the lights which have been placed about the altar, then those on the altar itself. As the last is put out, say:

The rite is ended.

X. SOLITARY RITE FOR THE AUTUMN EQUINOX

One should dress brightly, in "Autumn" colors, for this rite. As in other seasonal rites the robe, gown, or other apparel worn for this ceremony should be magical and "witchy" in its cut and feel. The altar should be set up as usual, shortly after dark, and with autumn leaves placed on and about it. Place also some fruits and vegetables on and about the altar, some of which will be eaten near the end of the ritual. Wine (or fruit juice) and a glass or goblet are to be placed before the altar. A large candle should be placed at either side of the altar. A broom (old-fashioned, if possible) should be laid just to the east of the altar, and a small pile of autumn leaves placed just to the west of the altar.

Before dressing for this rite one should bathe, bearing strongly in mind that as the physical water about you washes away all physical impurities, so also does the spiritual water cleanse your heart and soul.

When you are prepared, meditate for a while on the golden autumn, not only of the year, but of man's lives, of nations, of whole civilizations . . . the bright and warm flame that "flares impossibly bright" before fading away into darkness . . . to return again in times to come. When you feel ready, go to the place of ritual and stand briefly before the altar. In your mind, frame works of greeting to the Lady and to Her sturdy consort, The Horned God.

Light the candles, then take the leaves and, starting at the west, spread them clockwise in a circle about the altar and yourself. Then take the broom and draw it in a circle just within the circle of leaves, starting at the west, about the altar and yourself, ending at the west. Stand before the altar with your arms stretched out before you, and proclaim:

> As it was at the Time
> Of the beginning,
> So it is now!

Take the symbols of Water, of Earth, of Air, and of Fire . . . each in turn . . . "presenting" them over the altar, and saying for each:

> Goddess of the fields
> And God of the hunt,
> All power of the elements is yours.

At this time you may make such additions to the rite as you feel are appropriate. Playing a musical instrument or singing in honor of the Old Ones, or similar activities are proper. If such is your inclination, you may improvise a Dance and Procession of the Harvest, bearing in mind that mere plants can "sense" things also, so the harvest must be respectful to them. To close the rite, rap slowly five times upon the altar with the wand, and say:

78

The color of bracken does appear, as
the swan flies south.
Time passes, and I am here; for the
sanctuary I have built
Shall be about me, in spirit, for all
seasons. Blessed Be.

Put out the candles and sweep away the leaves with the
broom.

PART TWO

ADVANCED PAGAN RITUALS

☆ ☆ ☆

Paganism

Something very ancient ... yet very new and revolutionary to our society ... is beginning to appear on today's scene. Though a system of religion, it is as with Buddhism and Shinto, a philosophy and an intimate, person-to-person way of life. Its roots are deeper by far than that of Christianity and Judaism, stretching further back than any other European religion.

It is Paganism.

At this point in the century it is rather popular to say to each other that we have come to a new age. The old Piscean way of life is changing, and we are entering into the Aquarian age. Thanks to the modern theatre there are few who do not know that we are in a time of change.

It isn't necessary to read a book on astrology to know we are in a transition. One only needs to read the newspaper or listen to a conversation on the bus on the way to work. Our political climate, our racial views, our science, our family structure, all have drastically changed in less than the span of one life time. The list is endless. There seems to be no end or peace of mind for anyone. Everything is being examined. Everything seems unstable. Political pressures fashion the wonders of science into fearsome weapons. Commercialism, in its mindless striving for money, has managed to prostitute the finest technical developments and through their waste to pollute much of what still remains of the natural world. Still, for the first time, the entire western world is protesting war. The U.S., poisoning itself for so many years, is being directed toward a nationwide ecological program that may, hopefully, change the face of the globe.

The established major religions are greatly weakened and failing in their duty to man, for their foundations have been largely destroyed by a rapidly changing world. Mostly they have failed to grow with the submerged spiritual man.

The aim of the pagan movement, now and in the past, has been to unite man with the tidal harmony of the cosmos. In the Early Christian religion the church endeavored to eliminate the man/nature/unity principle as expressed in the ritual. The early church was in competition with the disorganized and failing Pagan religions. At that time, the Pagans were experiencing much the same conditions we are now experiencing, the end of an era. The established religion was much the same as the established religion now. It could not cope with the changing times because it had not evolved with humanity as we progressed along the path.

The leaders of the early church attempted to kill the spirit of nature in man, the worship of the planets and the forces they represented, but they soon found complete transgression is impossible, and as most new religions do, it attempted to absorb the old, keeping what it considered the best and eliminating the bad. So in the old church we have a slight change in the festivals: they were no longer called astrological, but nevertheless were. The Goddess became the Virgin. The Sun God became the Christ. The lesser and local gods became the saints. The language of the ritual changed, but the meaning did not. Man was still a part of the Gods.

This change of the astrological age continued through the Protestant reformation and followed the death of the ritualistic observation of the cosmic rhythm soon after that. This was followed by the age of reason of the nineteenth century and the scientific machine age producing materialism never experienced by mankind. Social orders grew in a pattern that moved away from nature and cosmic rhythm, rather than toward it.

Man responded to the patterns he was creating. His life became unnecessarily complex until seemingly almost overnight we were involved in such a complicated method of relationships that relationship itself had no meaning. Science became so self reliant that god, or whatever man has called god, was discarded. Nature, under the exposing but limiting microscope became clusters of cells without the overall pattern of meaning. Reason itself became unreasonable.

The result is and continues to be inevitable. Social systems and psychological systems that are based upon crumbling spiritual values, or disassociated social systems, result in total disruption of society pitted against itself in the game we call war. The Protestant insistence of man abandoning his ties with the patterned universe resulted in our aligning ourselves with cultures or leaders who seemed to give us that which we no longer received from our religion. These leaders, uniting themselves with Chaos, have led us to the brink, and there we stand. It is fortunate that we have at least moved into the new age, and if we can quickly align ourselves with the Universal principle, then we shall survive.

The dark picture is not encompassing. The answer lies deep within ourselves . . . and out in the world of nature where it has long waited. If you can relax enough to seek the wooded paths or go to the water's edge, you can feel the power that is within you, and that is the power of the universe itself.

The age-old lore also exists in folk beliefs. It is in the dusty books of the magician, and in the wisdom of the practices of the Craft. It is in the rituals of the ancient Christian way, and preserved by small underground groups since the time of the persecution.

The Pagan Way is very close to the soul of Humanity, it is a natural belief which sees man as he is, and the world as it is, and seeks to push neither into a preconceived model. Paganism sees the mystery and richness of nature, and opens the way to an understanding of it, that the modern world has overlooked.

There are some beliefs that pagans share in common which are somewhat different from that of other humans.

A Pagan refuses to believe that mankind is born innately sinful, and realizes that the concept of "Sin" is harmful to human nature.

He realizes the powers of the universe, sometimes called "God," exist, not apart, but as *part* of man.

These powers may be contacted ,directed, and benefit may be gained from them; if man first learns to live in harmony with himself and the universe.

The movement of these natural forces, called "tides" by many, directly affect our lives, the evolution of humanity, and the course of the manifested universe.

The Pagan celebrates this force movement, in fact unifies with it, through the calendar of the year which we call the greater and lesser festivals.

These festivals are attuned to the tides, and also reflect the eternal problems of man as he has moved forward upon the path of light.

The Pagan recognizes, and harmonizes with, the law of nature called polarity.

We know that "that which is above is as that which is below."

There is no heaven except that which we ourselves make, and likewise there is no hell.

Harmony with and direction of the great natural forces is called magic.

We know that the basis of the natural forces is the Supernal Intelligence, reflected in all Gods, and reflected in man, is also within all creation.

Paganism is not fixed nor dogmatic.

We know of the existence of the spark of life that is within us that does not die, and that returns again and again until it has evolved to that which we call the eternal existence above all existences.

We abide by the great rule of love, and that one may do as he wishes as long as it harms no other.

Nature is ourselves, and to harm it is to cut off an arm or leg of our own body. Therefore we support ecology and do all that we can to regrow the forests and renew the seas.

At this time overpopulation is the plague of mankind, from which many of our troubles arise. The Pagan is obligated to restrain from producing that which he cannot support.

We must return to the old ones, for it is there that we exist, and it is from that place that the psychology of our lives emerge. To ignore the nature that is ourselves is to cause life to leave our bodies leaving only shells in the place of that which was once human.

The Gods

We give honor to many Gods in the Pagan Way. It must be immediately realized that these many Gods are the Many Forms of the One God, the great force that lies behind all creation. The closest that philosophers have come to a definition of the One is "A state of Pure Being." Not a force that is "good." Not a force that is "bad." Not a force that is dark or light, but an existence that simply "IS."

Now this Oneness is not only nature, but it is the Supreme Power that transcends all of the Universe. So Providence, the bountiful one, creator of all things, is the material universe, but also above that universe. As you will now appreciate, the One stands beyond the range of the human mind, as it is the inmost self of all things, and may only be perceived in the mirror of the universe. Thus the knowledge of the One is attained only through the symbols and laws It has created.

The apparent form of the One that we may understand is the Truth of polarity. Everything is dual; everything has two poles; everything has its pair of opposites. Opposites are identical in nature but different in degree. This great truth we express in the form of the male/female aspect of polarity, the God and the Goddess. In terms of a creation theory, the One is both male and female, being all things. As creation comes about through the conjunction of the male and the female the One immediately may be represented by a second level consisting of male and female figures, the God and the Goddess.

The God and Goddess are not mere symbols of the God, except as everything is symbolic. They are representatives in the physical universe of principles that are as near to the One that we may experience and still remain human.

These principles are personified during the solar year and have assumed many forms in many traditions. Different peoples have called the God and the Goddess many names. All the names are the true name, for it matters not what they are called.

Throughout history, the four seasons have symbolized man's journey through life. In the Spring the pregnant Goddess of nature emerges from the underworld when melting snow signals the bursting of the divine placenta. The infant God of the year is born at the Spring equinox, and after the delivery the Goddess again becomes a maiden. Beltane marks full adolescence and the engagement of the young God and Goddess as pollination begins. Midsummer marks their wedding feast: the year's orgasm beginning on the longest day of the year. The embryo of the coming year develops around Lammas, August 1, with the ripening fruit. The Autumnal equinox and the harvest moon, the brightest of the year, signal relaxation and release as the fruits fall. Halloween ushers the return of the dead and the descent into the underworld. At the Winter solstice, the longest night of the year, the Holy Infant thrusts from within the womb of the Goddess the seeds of the new year received from the God of the preceeding year. He will be born at the next Vernal Equinox to become her lover once more.

We celebrate this yearly process with the Agricultural and Zodiacal festivals of the year.

The Goddess has three stages representing Her, according to the time of the year and the stage of the moon. The Virgin maiden corresponds to the waxing moon, the Bountiful mother corresponds to the full moon, and the Hag of death corresponds to the waning moon.

The God has two aspects corresponding to the sun: The Lord of Light corresponding to the day, and the Lord of Death and Resurrection corresponding to the night.

As the balance of night and day alter through the year, so one or the other aspects of the God and Goddess become dominant.

The Universe is created and held together in being by the conjunction of these two aspects of the Creator, and together with the Creator, they lie beyond creation.

Different but not separate from the God and Goddess are other powers that have god-like qualities. These are usually common in nature and have over long periods of human name-tagging become as gods in our minds. They are aspects of the One and the Two. Some of these different types of gods are dwellers on other planes that we are able to contact, and in our ignorance we call them Gods. In a way they are God-like as far as humans are concerned, but they too are limited by the laws of the planes on which they live. It is our duty to attempt to understand these contacts and give them their proper treatment, not worshiping them as Gods.

Another all-too-common god is the one we create when we meet natural powers that are stronger than ourselves. Some of these, like the lightning and thunder gods of primitive peoples are easily understood, but the natural emissions of planets and stars and their effect upon our personality is a bit more subtle. We find that as the old religions began to disintegrate the natural more refined cosmic forces became gods also. It is error to believe that the effects of the solar rays are God. It is error to worship the moon, except where that veneration is directed to God himself through the marvels of his creation. Simply because we are awed by nature does not mean that it is to be worshipped.

A cosmic force without an astral form is not a god; and a god form ensouled without cosmic force is not a god either. When a cosmic force of a pure type is embodied in an astral thought form we have what is called an Artificial Elemental. In some faiths this is called a god and in others an archangel.

These thought-forms are creations of the group, race, or social actions of groups of men. They act over long periods of time in a specified direction and the result of their rituals creates, on the astral plane, an embodied thought-form.

A God in this case, then, is an Artificial Elemental of a very powerful type, built up over long periods of time by successive generations whose minds were cast in the same mold. It is therefore a form of such potency that no evocator can hope to dominate it in the way he would an elemental of his own creation. He must yield himself to its influence and permit it to dominate him if it is to be evoked to visible manifestation. The operator himself is the channel of evocation. It is in his imagination that the image of both god and elemental builds itself up, and it is the corresponding aspect of his own nature which provides the ensouling force. In the case of an Elemental, however, the whole of the force is derived subjectively; but in the case of a god, objective, racial, cosmic force passes through the corresponding aspect of the workers' nature to ensoul the form. It is well to note that this sort of Elemental is capable of control of entire sections and indeed the more power that is poured into the Elemental the more control it has. Hence very powerful God aspects last many thousands of years and their effects can be felt at their temple sites long after the ritual has ceased to be worked. Others, working long after the ending of particular faiths can make contact with the deity and affect results even though thousands of years have passed.

It is to the advantage of the pagan to build personal temples where regular ritual is worked. We may draw from these sources power for ourselves and others though we must know what we are doing and how. It is of the utmost importance that the modern Pagan fully understands the religious paths he pursues.

The Degrees

There are five basic Pagan degrees, corresponding to the elemental path toward unity with the Godhead. Added to this is the neophyte degree, corresponding to the time the neo-pagan begins to study The Path until the time of his first initiation. The Circle is open to the neophyte but he may not participate in the eucharist, initiations, or major festivals. Thus we have:

> First Degree — *Earth*
> Second Degree — *Air*
> Third Degree — *Fire*
> Fourth Degree — *Water*
> Fifth Degree — *Akasha* or *Spirit*

The degrees correspond with the four basic magical types of man — the Thinking, the Feeling, the Sensing and the Intuitional.

(a). *Thinking Man (Fire)* This type classifies, analyses, synthesizes, argues from premise to conclusion, traces the reason for this and that.

(b). *Feeling Man (Water)* This type also makes judgments, but in a totally different way. He is not concerned with reasons, but with the value. The standard by which he measures is not logic but worth. "This I like," he says, "That I do not like. This is good. That is bad. This is morally right. That is morally wrong."

(c). *Sensation Man (Earth)* This type, like the intuitional type, works by perception, but works entirely in the field of facts, and nothing but facts. It (perception) sees what is and what is not. Its weakness is that it cannot conceive of any other way in which one may look at life.

(d). *Intuitional Man (Air)* This type, like the Sensation man, works by perception, but in this case the perception is of something beyond the facts — the imponderables, the intangible important possibilities, the events beyond the horizon and the shape of things to come.

Spiritual man is the man who has mastered all the facets of the other four aspects. It is true that within ourselves exist all these qualities, but it is the Spiritual man who has brought them to the surface, and integrated them into his personality, able to command their usage at will.

There are colors assigned to the five degrees. Robes, cords, clothing at festivals and other color coordinated items should be of the color of the degree. If black robes are chosen, and they are recommended because of the general usage, then Lamens, and other items of accent, should be of the color of the degree.

> Earth — *Yellow*
> Air — *Blue*
> Fire — *Red*
> Water — *Silver*
> Spirit— *Black or Indigo*

The traditional Tattwa symbols are associated with the degrees: Earth, Square; Air, Circle or disc; Fire, Triangle; Water, Crescent — points up; Spirit, Egg-shape.

During the time in the First degree, the Pagan must learn what his life path is to be and how to keep himself upon it. It is the degree of the purification of the mind and body. He must set himself on the road of self understanding and correct all habits and faults that obstruct him from uniting with nature as represented in the ritual. He must harmonize the qualities within himself so communication is possible with the cosmic forces. This is no easy task. For many it is a long period of introspection, and for this reason no time is set for the First degree. He is expected to know mythology and to understand its inner meaning to himself, but also to others as the myths apply to humanity as a whole. Symbols and tools are to be understood, constructed, and used.

Much of the work described above is work that is directed to the inner self, and once the centers are open to the powers, the motion is set, and the inner self gains much from the ritual and from the greater outer universe using psychic methods removed from seemingly "actual" work. However, the path must be first opened directly by the worker, and it is to this that the first degree is dedicated.

Devotion – Invocation – Evocation – Prayer

As Pagans we must always remember devotion is directed to the human self as well as to the God forces in general. All that is without in the great physical universe is also continued in the smaller universe, the inner self. All invocation, evocation, prayer, in fact, devotionals of any kind must interact upon both universes, the macrocosm (outer universe) and the microcosm (inner universe).

This section of the first degree is to teach the student to use the various levels of devotion, not to think about them. Devotion must be approached emotionally, with the whole self, not through the mind alone.

The Gods are most quickly approached through the emotions. It is through this impact that we are able to direct those great natural forces to aid ourselves and to aid humanity in general.

Directed changes in the inner or outer levels of the human attract the natural forces of the universe to ourselves. Invocation, evocation, and prayer are the most usual methods of directing this power.

Invocation is an action designed to attract some being, spirit, or force to ourselves whose nature is greater or superior to our own.

Evocation is the emotion of impelling our actions or wishes upon other types of existence whose levels of development are less than our own.

Prayer is the method to bring together within ourselves the realization and identification of the forces that exist in ourselves. It is the mobilization of the qualities of the self into a working recognition of the god forces or natural forces of the universe.

These ideas are recognized in the inner self thus causing changes in that inner self which produces contact with the forces themselves.

Devotion is the method of implanting channels into the inner self for those outer forces to enter into the self, and the inner forces to exit into the conscious self, thus producing conscious self recognition of the natural or god forces existent in the universe.

Meditation

We are establishing a method of receiving these messages in such a way that they are completely under control, and are received as realizations, and as changes in complete attitudes, rather than as visions. At all times it will be possible for the student to return to the physical worlds.

Meditation is recommended in the morning, after rising, before dressing.

Use one spot, free of noise, that you can use for no other purpose.

If a robe is available, wear it during meditation, and at no other time.

Temples, robes, incense, chants and the like are methods used to ease the entry into the other worlds, and exit from this.

A salutation at noon to the Sun is recommended to remind the student of his attachment to nature, and to help him to begin to return to that from whence he came.

Records of all meditations are absolutely necessary.

In the evening, review the entire day in bed, before falling asleep, as simple bare statements, from morning to evening.

The Method of Meditation

There are various forms of meditation but one which we are concerned with first is the technique of holding an idea in the mind and following trains of thought from it, but not in such a way that one is led far astray from the original subject. The mind should be brought back to the main idea as soon as it begins to drift too far away. Irrelevant ideas or images in the mind should be cast out without examination or delay.

In this manner the mind circles round and about a key idea — the subject of the meditation — and, as it were, bores a well down through the layer of the mentality to the subconscious mind. Persistently pursued, deeper levels than the personal unconscious appear.

Rhythmic Breathing

The exercises in realization lead on to the use of the rhythmic breath and should be reasonably well mastered before going on to it. Rhythmic breathing will be found to improve the powers of relaxation already gained. It also stills and concentrates the mind as a basis for later visualization work apart from making available an increase of psychic energy and etheric vitality — to say nothing of the beneficial physical effects, as most of us use our lungs inefficiently most of the time.

The important thing to watch for here is not to strain, nor to hold the breath, in or out, by an inhibitory effect of will. There must be no forced effect. The air should be taken in to the bottom of the lungs first by the simple method of pushing the abdomen out (*i.e.,* the diaphragm down) and thus causing the air to be sucked naturally into the lungs until they are filled to the top.

Again, there should be no forced retention of the breath with consequent strain on lung tissue, but the air should be retained for the requisite time by holding the diaphragm down and the chest wall out. If the chest is tapped sharply it should cause part of the air to be expelled, thus proving that there is no barrier in the throat or mouth.

To breathe out, suck the abdomen in (*i.e.*, the diaphragm up) so that the air is expelled naturally and is felt to leave the top of the lungs last of all. Keep the breath held out by use of the diaphragm and trunk muscles.

For general purposes, we use the technique known as the fourfold breath. Inhale slowly to a count of eight; retain the breath to a count of four; exhale at the same speed to a count of eight; hold the lungs empty to a count of four.

Alternatively, once can count four and two, or six and three, or whatever seems most comfortable according to one's individual constitution, speed of counting and breathing, and lung capacity. The important thing is avoidance of strain or "overbreathing," giving symptoms of dizziness.

Planetary Knowledge

The planets represent the driving forces of life.

PLANET	FORCE	SIGN
Sun	Self integration, individuality	☉
Moon	Rhythm, personality	☽
Mercury	Communicative reason	☿
Venus	Uniting, social activities	♀
Mars	Activity, dynamic energy	♂
Jupiter	Expansion, vision idealism	♃
Saturn	Formation through restriction	♄
Uranus	Deviation through invention	♅
Neptune	Refining, occultism	♆
Pluto	Transformation	♇

The Zodiac

Aries, the Ram; Taurus, the Bull; Gemini, the Twins; Cancer, the Crab; Leo, the Lion; Virgo, the Virgin; Libra, the Scales; Scorpio, the Scorpion; Sagittarius, the Archer; Capricorn, the Goat; Aquarius, the Water-bearer; Pisces, the Fish.

Each sign is attributed to one of the four Elemental Signs. They are:

FIRE	**EARTH**	**AIR**	**WATER**
Aries	Virgo	Gemini	Cancer
Leo	Taurus	Libra	Scorpio
Sagittarius	Capricorn	Aquarius	Pisces

Fundamental Buddhist Teachings

Eight steps to Enlightenment:

1. Right Knowledge
2. Right Speech
3. Right Aims
4. Right Conduct
5. Right Means of Livelihood
6. Right Effort
7. Right Attention
8. Right Concentration

Elements

Elements of the Ancients

    Heat and Dryness — *Fire*
    Heat and Moisture — *Air*
    Cold and Dryness — *Earth*
    Cold and Moisture — *Water*

Four Orders of the Elementals
    Spirits of the Earth — *Gnomes*
    Spirits of the Air — *Sylphs*
    Spirits of the Water — *Undines*
    Spirits of the Fire — *Salamanders*

The information in this chapter is elemental. It is applied and reapplied throughout your experience upon the plane. In following grades more instruction booklets will be issued, including more advanced information. In all cases it will be based upon the method and basic material available in this booklet. It is suggested that you apply the material as fully as possible. Some of it may not be used for several years, but all eventually shall. Remember, the first degree is the degree of learning and purification. Lessons, brought into yourself using the meditation methods described herein, are never lost, and are always available when needed. In the classes we shall become familiar with such things as Gnomes and Salamanders. For the time being, take into yourself the information listed here. Have it ready to recall when needed.

Ritual Influences of the Days of the Week

Sunday

The Sun
Perfumes: Heliotrope, Orange Blossom, Cloves, Frankincense, Ambergris, Musk, Myrrh
Incense: Mastic, Palaginia
Wood: Laurel
Color: Orange, Gold
Influences: Health, Healing, Confidence and Hope, Prosperity

Monday

The Moon
Perfume: White Poppy, White Rose, Wallflower
Incense: Myrtle
Wood: Willow
Color: Silver, Grey-white
Influences: Agriculture, Domestic, Longlife, Medicine, Travels, Visions, Theft (new moon)

Tuesday

Mars
Perfume: Hellebore, Carnation, Patchouli
Incense: Lignum Aloes, Plantain
Color: Red
Influences: Destination, War, Courage, Surgery, Physical Strength

Wednesday

Mercury
Perfumes: Sweetpea, Lavender, Mastic, Frankincense, Cloves
Incense: Cinnamon, Cinquefoil
Color: Yellow or Grey
Influences: Conjurations, Predictions, Knowledge, Writing, Eloquence

Thursday

Jupiter
Perfumes: Stock, Lilac, Storax, Aloes
Incense: Nutmeg, Henbane

Wood: Pine
Color: Purple, Indigo, Blue
Influences: Luck, Religion, Healing, Trade and Employment, Treasure, Honors, Riches, Legal Matters

Friday

Venus
Perfumes: Stephanotis, Apple Blossom, Musk, Ambergris
Incense: Saffron, Verbena
Wood: Myrtle
Color: Light Blue, Pale Green
Influences: All Love Matters, Friendships, Affection, Partnerships, Money, Sex

Saturday

Saturn
Perfumes: Hyacinth, Pansy
Incense: Peperwort, Assodilious, Black Poppy Seeds, Henbane, Lodestone, Myrrh
Wood: Oak
Color: Black
Influences: Duties, Respondibilities, Finding Families, Works of Magic, Buildings, Meditation, Life, Doctrines.

It should be noted that whatever work is performed, the moon should be of paramount importance and it should be noted whether it is waxing or waning, as the Wicca is a moon cult. But if the work performed be in good auspices with both moon and day and the correct incense, etc., this is to your advantage.

Healing

Much of what will be said in this chapter can be generalized to apply to other types of magical work as well as to healing. To a large extent the methods are basically similar; the difference being in the ultimate change one wants to bring about. Thus, on a broader scale, the following will also be a treatise on magick in general.

In healing and other magical work the concept of "power" is mentioned frequently. This power is, basically, an energy that one uses, harnesses, and directs, in order to bring about the desired effects. This power exists on different levels, and may be used on one level or another, or in combination, depending on the task to be accomplished and the way a particular healer feels he can best work. There is a type of power that is "of the gods," the force discussed in the chapter on paganism. As briefly stated in that chapter, magical work depends on the ability to contact, direct and utilize this power, and in order to do this one must be in tune with the harmony of the whole universe. In Spiritualistic and other circles one often hears people speak of healing as being "magnetic" or "divine." Divine healing consists of the use of this power from the higher sources.

The force we are talking about exists throughout the universe. The Yogis call it prana. The Psychiatrist Wilhelm Reich called it orgone energy. Baron Von Reichenbach referred to it as odic force. It is also known by other names. To all who have studied this power it is known to exist both within and without the human body. As just stated, on the highest level this force emanates from, also IS, the Divine, Absolute, Source, Great Unmanifest, Logos, or whatever term one chooses to refer to the ultimate level of existence.

Everything that exists above also exists below and everyone who has studied and worked with this power has recognized its presence both within us, emanating from us and in the cosmos. Our own states of vitality or lack of it are a function of this circulation of force within us. Both the etheric double and the aura of the human body are composed to a large extent of this power, and a person who is in a vibrant, highly charged state, by virtue of personal well-being and/or occult work will be able to project a considerable amount of this power from himself. It is the use of power on this level that is known as magnetic healing.

One cannot say that one type of healing or the other is more valid, or that it shows greater evidence of a person's state of "spiritual evolution." For certain types of work one use of force may be appropriate, for another something else. As mentioned before there is often a blending of that which is from within and that which is from without.

Beginning healers, or magicians in general, should focus much of their attention to the direction of this power. Exercises aimed at direction should precede the actual work. There is an important principle here: power manifests where attention is directed. Meditate on this, ask questions about it, see if you can prove this statement to your own satisfaction. Make this concept a part of yourself; it is a primary ingredient in magical work. One beginning exercise is to concentrate your thought on various parts of your body, one part at a time. See if you feel the power. How do you experience it? When you have mastered this, concentrate the power by directing the attention outside of yourself. Stare at the back of the head of a stranger, on a bus, on the street, in a meeting, etc. In many instances the power will be felt and the person will turn around to you. If you're anxious to leave a restaurant and want to get the waiter or waitress' attention, stare in the appropriate direction and project the thought of the check being brought to you. It beats yelling across the room. You can also begin to project ideas into objects, to magnetically load them with some suitable thought. An example would be in the making of a talisman.

If there is any difficulty in feeling the power as it emanates from oneself a good method is to practice the "accordion" exercise. Hold your hands in front of you about two feet apart, then slowly bring them together, then slowly apart again, and so on. When you are bringing your hands together, note the point at which you begin to feel a resistance, a sensation that something is pushing back — like two magnets being pushed toward each other. It is that sensation that is the power from the etheric body. Practice with another person, so that you can each feel the power emanating from the other's hands. Due to the laws of polarity one can generally experience this more intensely in working with a person of the opposite sex.

It will take a little longer to experience the power as it comes from and through the Cosmos. This is generally best experienced in a situation of magical ritual. One must first learn to experience the magnetic force as it comes from himself and from other people. As mentioned before, the projection of this force depends in part upon the individual's state of personal vitality and also on his ability to understand the nature of the magnetic energy to be attuned to it and to direct it outside of himself. Since it is partly contingent on the state of personal well-being, it is important to state that the would-be healer or magician eat a diet composed largely of natural, unprocessed food and in general follow a way of life conducive to good health.

In order to avoid confusion we must restate that we are talking primarily of power coming from two principle sources — the force of the gods, and that which exists within oneself and can be directed outwards. Actually, this exists more on a continuum rather than as either-or, but for convenience of expression it is permissible to think of it in terms of Divine or Magnetic, or that which is above or below, without or from within. Healing work can further be divided into two categories — contact and absent or distant. In the former, the person to be healed is where you are, and in the latter he is not present. As is true of telepathy and other forms of psychism, healing power knows no boundaries. It is just as possible to heal someone distantly who is in the next room as it is to give this sort of aid to a person who is in another country. To some extent, but not to any absolute degree, one tends to use more of the magnetic sort of healing power when helping someone who is present, and to use more of the so-called Divine type of power in working for a person who is absent from the ritual situation. However, this must only be taken as a relative, not an absolute, statement since the various levels of force generally enter into the healing situation in combination.

The amount of ritual can vary from a lot to a little. Beginners should tend to use a greater amount. It is also essential to use more ritual when the person you are working for is someone you don't know personally and may not have any emotional investment in. If you are working for someone close to you and have a deep personal desire to see that individual well again the emotional investment can in part substitute for the ritual. As an aside, it might be interesting to point out that this is the reason that magic done with the intent of harming someone often works more effectively than the so-called white magic does. That is, in seeking to do harm to another, to gain revenge, etc., there is usually a powerful reserve of emotion underlying the magical act. This emotion, coupled with ritual, makes for a potent combination insuring a relatively high likelihood of success. This is, therefore, why one can say that for an experienced healer, especially where there is a very strong personal investment in helping the patient, emotion can be a partial substitute for the ritual. Basically, when we speak of the use of ritual in healing we are talking of the sort of work when the person is not present.

In doing a healing where the patient is in attendance, there should be less ritual magical work; rather the emphasis would be on projecting power into him. In order to best accomplish this, the healer's hands should be about two inches away from the skin. We are working on the subtle force of the etheric body, not the physical body. Disease is first registered in the etheric body, and it is on this double of the physical self that we aim healing power. The hands can be held over the afflicted area of the body in order to implant magnetic vitality, as well as moved about the body to "comb out" the etheric, as it were. Downward strokes of the hands should be used to induce a state of relaxation and calm. Upward strokes add vitality. The hands can be used to "draw out" the diseased condition and once this is done magnetism of a healthier sort can be replaced. When drawing out diseased etheric matter, the healer should snap his fingers in a direction away from the patient in order to rid himself of it; otherwise the healer could find himself taking on the condition he is curing the patient of. Some practitioners prefer using a bowl of water as a receptacle for diseased etheric matter. Each healer will develop his style of working.

No two healers practice the exact same way. The information presented here is a general guideline, but allows much variation in practice.

Most practitioners of healing will find that when they are emanating the power one hand seems warmer and one seems colder. The warmer hand is the one of positive polarity and in most people is the right hand. Conversely, the left hand usually embodies negative polarity. In many instances of healing the positive hand should be placed over the area where the disease exists and the negative hand on the other side, allowing the power to flow through from positive to negative and vice-versa.

Since the majority of healing work done in witchcraft and pagan Circles is of the distant or absent variety, most of the discussion will be focused on this. Most people think of pagan groups as doing a considerable amount of chanting and Circle dancing. This is true. These methods are pleasurable and impart a sense of joy and communion with nature to the meetings, so are desirable from that standpoint alone, but they are also time-honored means of "raising the power." In a practicing craft or general pagan Circle, power will have to be raised in order to do healing, to work to end the war, to stop animal abuse, to help persons avoid being drafted into the military, to promote ecology, etc. No matter what the goal, the power must be raised.

Some groups feel that nudity is a vital prerequisite for raising the power. The writer has worked nude, wearing street clothes and in robes and feels that it is the intent and cohesion of the group that governs whether power can be successfully generated and directed, not the absence of clothing. The arguments in favor of nudity as it relates to power is that clothing supposedly blocks the force from emanating from the body. Since the power can be successfully directed across oceans to heal persons in other countries, one can immediately see that this argument is invalid. Also, most practitioners experience the magnetic emanations as being strongest in the palms of the hands and from the forehead.

Such details as robes, incense, candles, music, chanting and dancing are not necessary to success, but do serve as a focus for the mind in directing the power that these same things help to raise. It is much easier to use these external devices than to attempt to work by merely mental means alone. The altar and the ritual tools, the music, etc., further, have a conditioning effect on the mind, so that they come to be associated with the type of work to be done. With these stimuli available one can readily train oneself to direct the power in the desired directions. An additional advantage is that the desired vibratory magnetism can be accumulated in these objects.

Robes are helpful in that they are garments used solely for the purpose of the ritual work and when you enter the robe you enter a different world, or a different state of being. If one does not possess a robe then it is essential to have a special garment set aside for ritual purpose or to at least dress a little differently than one does for ordinary events of the day. All of this will be discussed in more detail in another section.

Music should be of a fairly primitive sort, something that will evoke feelings of a kinship with nature. Music can be on records or on tape, or members of the group can play simple instruments, such as the flute, recorder, drum, thumb piano, etc. Dancing, which shall also be discussed in another section, should be of a simply, folk type, again expressive of our kinship with nature. Chanting, either general chants, or those devised to suit the situaion you are working on, are also very helpful. These methods are all aimed at bringing out the power that is raised from within the individual members of the Circle. Once enough power is generated, it must then be directed toward the desired end.

For this purpose a "focus" is needed. This may be an object belonging to the person being helped, a photograph, or some of his hair or fingernails. The latter may conjure up images of evil magic, but it is important to remember that in working for good or evil, the methods are pretty similar; what is different is the intent. Any of these objects will be helpful in establishing a magnetic link with the person being helped. This is why the power is directed into the object. If none is available, the power is then aimed toward the person directly. Again, it is the desire to help, rather than the details of the method, which is the crucial factor. One may wonder why and how an object serves as a magnetic link. By way of a very brief explanation some thing that belongs to a person, or some part of his body (as hair or nails, or even a drop of blood) contains within it the vibratory essence of that person, and through the object you can contact the person. The interested reader is referred to a study of the principles underlying the science of radionics. It is a belief among African Witchdoctors that if a person is bitten by a snake, the first thing to do is kill that snake, because by doing so the magnetic link between the snake and his venom in the victim is broken. They believe that no matter what you do to aid the victim, results will be poor unless the snake is killed.

Sympathetic magic may also be used along with the focus of magnetic linkage. Thus, a wax image, or even a cloth image or a simple drawing of the person can be made. To these images can be affixed the hair, nails, photograph, etc. Also, one can add substances known to be curative to the condition on a physical level. As an example, the writer once made a wax image of a person about to undergo emergency surgery for a bleeding ulcer. To this image, in the abdominal region, some milk and some vitamin C were added. Also a scarf belonging to the patient was sacrificed to the element of fire. This was coupled with an intense projection of group mind force, along with chanting and dancing. Needless to say, the healing was a total success, the patient experiencing it while it was happening, although not knowing work was being done for her at that time.

In addition to the creation of images, sympathetic magic can also be done through the use of acting out that which you hope to accomplish. For example, in working for a person who has some sort of disorder that would make walking difficult, the group could go around the circle moving about with precise coordination, the attempt being made to transfer at least some of this ability to the person being healed.

Sometimes, the group will not use this sort of magic, but will do some dancing and chanting and then when the power is used will direct into the object of focus, aiming the hands at this. Or, as mentioned before, the power can be directed toward the person. It helps, incidentally, to know the person's full name and the condition he is suffering from. If full information is not available, results can sometimes be obtained, on the strength of the group's collective intent and through the ability of the God and Goddess to know where the power needs to be sent.

Getting into a discussion of the more spiritual aspects of healing (remember this is not either-or, actually both are used in combination, generally) a ritual is begun with an invocation to the God and Goddess, asking them to descend in power to the group and to help with the work to be done. This is a general invocation, a bringing down of the God power. Wording for this can come from already-written invocation, or one can word it as he feels it should be worded at the time of making the invocation.

After a general invocation is made, whoever is presenting a person to be healed will make a specific request to the God and Goddess pertaining to that situation. It is in the beginning invocation that much of the power from the Divine sources is drawn down, or "earthed." If this is done successfully, within a tightly formed Circle, a change in the energy field of the room will be noted. This, in combination with the power that is raised from the members of the group, will provide a potent charge to the Circle.

If one wishes to work more in tone with the spiritual forces on a healing and not use a magnetic focus or any sympathetic magic, or even dancing, music or chanting, one need merely make the request to the God and Goddess and then the group stands in a circle around the altar and everyone raises his arms up high and allows this power to descend into him and then he directs it out to the desired end. One may ask why the power needs to flow through the group, why can't it just go from the God and Goddess to the sick individual. This is a hard question to answer. No doubt some of the spiritual forces is thusly directed, but the healing group is also serving as a channel for this force, and thereby does bring it down to earth level and subsequently re-directs it to those who need it.

There is no "best" method. Many covens and related Circles use a combination of these methods, perhaps blending power from the different levels of existence for each healing, but mixing and matching such means as pure meditation, sympathetic magic, dancing, etc. It seems as though the group's interest is heightened if the methods are varied.

What does one concentrate on during the actual healing ritual? Again, there is no one "best" way. It is important to state that visualisation is necessary. This is why a photograph can be very helpful. You might want to visualize the ill person in a state of well-being. Those who are more clinically minded might want to visualize the condition of disease in the body or mind and strive to right that. Another method is to create an astral temple and put the patient there for the healing. If this method is being used, it is important to build up a consistent image and use it for all healings. When a group has worked together for a long time and has built up a good sense of rapport, everyone might want to cooperate in the joint building of an astral temple. For this, a good painting or drawing of that which has been mutually built up will be essential, as a focus to insure consistency of imagery. The reader can meditate on the possible reasons why the creation of an astral healing temple might yield the best sort of healing results. It should be stated that all three types of visualization mentioned here can be used simultaneously.

The question might arise — why does healing work? This is a bit difficult to explain. Usually, one understands after a time through his own realizations. However, we might state that if we direct our emotion strongly toward some desired end we are releasing a very subtle, but potent force. If the emotion is directed toward a tangible end and accompanied by visual imagery, then a thought form is created. That is, the mental picture plus the outpouring of emotional force becomes a reality on the astral plane. This thought form which is actually a reality on the astral plane begins to give off its own vibrations and comes to become a cause of the desired effect in the person for whom help is being sought. Through continued practice of these methods certain inner plane "contacts" will be established who will also aid in the work.

Another explanation for the success of healings is that they can be done by telepathic influence, or telepathic hypnosis. One can speculate at great length on why magic works. Suffice it to say that it can and does work, and perhaps succeeds by virtue of more than one explanation.

It is sometimes difficult to evaluate healing success. Groups should be prepared to keep records, perhaps an index card with the person's name, problem, date(s) healing is given, and the results. It is best to work for people who are in contact with someone in the group, so you can check into the success or failure. The percentage of success depends on many factors: the intent and cohesion, as well as skill of the group, the type of problems healing is sought for, etc. Sometimes there is an immediate improvement, but one must check to see if there are other variables that could account for the success, such as the person getting well anyway, physical treatment given to the person, etc. In other instances, there is no other factor but healing to account for the patient's dramatic improvement.

One question often raised in discussions of healing concerns that of karma. Should we attempt to heal someone whose condition has been brought about due to his or her karma? This is often raised by people who aren't interested in doing healing; sometimes it is a searching attempt to evaluate whether healing should be done. While it may be true that much serious illness affecting mankind is karmic in nature, perhaps some of us have the obligation to help anyway. To play with words, one can say it is their karma to get sick, our karma to get them well. If the disease is karmic and the person is not "meant" to get well, no amount of healing will ever succeed. Therefore, we do not need to worry whether we will be affecting someone's karma when we do this sort of work.

Much of this discussion may seem a bit unclear at first, but should gradually have more meaning as you experience the different types of power and work the various methods of healing ritual.

☆ ☆ ☆

Herbs

The use of herbs has always been an integral part of the Craft of the Wise. Herbs can be used medicinally for humans and animals, as beverages, as cosmetics and as seasonings for food. Used medicinally, herbs definitely *do* bring about results, not as quickly as drugs (an increasing number of which are being synthesized from plant sources) but with fewer, if any, side effects. It is important to remember that the old-time practitioner of the pagan arts was, in addition to being an occult magician, a physician, mid-wife, and psychotherapist in the community. Thus, a good working knowledge of herbalism, as well as other means of treating disease through natural methods, was considered essential knowledge.

Many herbs, such as camomile, sassafras, mint, rose hips, fennel, linden, shave grass, sarsaparilla, fenugreek, parsley, elderberry, etc., make good-tasting teas and are enjoyable and healthful to drink. With regard to making herb teas, a general rule to follow is to use two teaspoons of the dried herb to one pint of boiling water. Let the tea steep 5 to 7 minutes.

Many persons interested in Witchcraft and Paganism want to know about "flying ointment." Some modern witches are experimenting with flying ointments, but these are dangerous brews to concoct either in a cauldron or in a modern cooking pot. The ointment, made of some rather toxic herbs, has powerful psychedelic effects. The tales about witches flying to sabbats on broomsticks seems to relate to the fact that flying ointments would often cause the user to etherically project and he or she might have the sensation of flying. Among the ingredients of flying ointment are: parsley, water of aconite, poplar leaves, soot, bat's blood, deadly nightshade, henbane, hashish, belladonna, hemlock and oil.

Flying ointment should be rubbed into the skin behind the ears, on the neck along the line of carotid arteries, in the armpits, to the left of the sympathetic nerve, in the bends of the knees and the arms and in the soles of the feet. After the application, the user should sleep naked in front of a fire or a statue of the Goddess.

The recipes vary according to the source. Before trying any experiments the reader is warned of the poisonous nature of some of the ingredients.

One of the most popular "witchy" herbs is Mugwort. Consumed as a tea, it is believed to facilitate clairvoyance. The crushed leaves, or juice, can also be rubbed on a crystal ball as a fluid condenser; Catnip is a time-honored sedative and is commonly given to babies in the southern states. Some good herbal tranquilizers are Valerian and Scullcap, made into a tea either singly or in combination. Raspberry leaf tea is used commonly to help render childbirth easier, and it is even given to women in labor in some British hospitals.

According to Sybil Leek, from her studies of Gypsy lore, dandelion is a laxative and a diuretic and is good in cases of diabetes, kidney troubles, and female disorders, as well as liver, spleen and pancreas difficulties. Many health food devotees drink ground dandelion roots as a coffee substitute. To test for pregnancy, place a few drops of urine on a big, course dandelion leaf. If red blisters appear on the leaf, the woman is pregnant.

Another useful multi-purpose herb is nettle. It is an excellent source of iron, so is helpful in anemia. It is also a blood purifier. The green leaves, steeped in water for a few hours, make an excellent poultice to relieve neuralgic pain. For rheumatism, rub the bruised leaves on the skin, and to stop bleeding, apply the boiled leaves externally.

Herbs *do* work. Over the past thirty years or so they have been supplanted in medical practice by drugs, because the latter do work more quickly and more dramatically, albeit often at great cost to the patient financially and in terms of side effects. Also, the use of natural healing methods isn't viewed as "scientific" by the AMA and other purveyors of "modern medicine." In England medical herbalism is a recognized profession and there must be several hundred practitioners. Training consists of an intensive course covering four years of study and clinical work.

The following is a glossary of terms used in herbalism. These words describe what the different types of herbs do and are used commonly.

ALTERNATIVE — A vague term to indicate a substance which hastens the renewal of tissues so that they can carry on their functions to better advantage.

ANODYNE — Pain-easing.

ANTHELMINITIC — Causing death or removal of worms in the body.

ANTIBILIOUS — Against biliousness.

ANTIPERIODIC — Preventing the return of those diseases which recur, such as Malaria.

ANTISCORBUTIC — Preventing Scurvey.

ANTISCROFULOUS — Preventing or curing scrofulous diseases.

ANTISEPTIC — Preventing putrefaction.

APERIENT — Producing a natural movement of the bowels.

APHRODISIAC — Exciting the sexual organs.

AROMATIC — Having an aroma.

ASTRINGENT — Binding. Causing contraction of the tissues.

BALSAMIC — Of the nature of a balsam. Usually applied to substances containing resins and benzoic acid.

BITTER — Applied to the bitter-tasting herbs which are used to stimulate the appetite.

CARDIAC — Properties which have an effect upon the heart.

CARMINATIVE — Easing gripping pains and expelling flatulence.

CATHARTIC — Producing evacuation of the bowels.

CHOLAGOGUE — Producing a flow of bile.

CORRECTIVE — Restoring to a healthy state.

DEMULCENT — Applied to herbs which soothe and protect the alimentary canal.

DEOBSTRUENT — Clearing away obstructions by opening the natural passages of the body.

DEPURATIVE — A purifying agent.

DERMATIC — Applied to herbs with an action on the skin.

DETERGENT — Cleansing.

DIAPHORETIC — Herbs which promote perspiration.

DIGESTIVE — Aiding digestion.

EMETIC — Applied to herbs which have the power of exciting the menstrual discharge.

EMOLLIENT — Used in relation to substances which have a softening and soothing effect.

EXPECTORANT — Promoting expectoration and removing secretions from the bronchial tubes.

FEBRIFUGE — Reducing fever.

HEMOSTATIC — Herbs used to control bleeding.

HEPATIC — Used in connection with substances having an effect on the liver.

HYDROGUE — Having the property of removing accumulations of water or serum. Causing watery evacuations.

HYPNOTIC — Producing sleep.

INSECTICIDE — Having the property of killing insects.

IRRITANT — Causing irritations.

LAXATIVE — A gentle bowel stimulant.

MYDRIATIC — Causing dilation of the pupil.

NARCOTIC — Applied to herbs producing stupor and insensibility.

NEPHRITIC — Herbs having an action upon the kidneys.

NERVINE — Applied to herbs used to restore the nerves to their natural state.

NUTRITIVE — Nourishing.

OXYTOCIC — Hastening birth by stimulating the contraction of the uterus.

PARASITICIDE — Destroying parasites.

PARTURIENT — Applied to substances used during childbirth.

PECTORAL — Used internally for afflictions of the chest and lungs.

PURGATIVE — Herbs which evacuate the bowels, more drastic than a laxative or aperient.

REFRIGERANT — Relieving thirst and giving a feeling of coolness.

RESOLVENT — A term used to denote substances applied to swellings in order to reduce them.

RUBEFACIENT — Applied to counter irritants. Substances which produce blisters or inflammation.

SEDATIVE — Herbs which calm nervous excitement.

STERNUTATORY — Producing sneezing by irritation of the mucous membrane.

STIMULANT — Energy producing.

STOMACHIC — Applied to herbs given for disorders of the stomach.

STYPTIC — Substances which clot the blood and thus stop bleeding.

SUDORIFIC — Producing copious perspiration.

TAENICIDE — Applied to drugs used to expel tape-worms.

TONIC — Substances which give tone to the body producing a feeling of well-being.

VERMIFUGE — Substances which expel worms from the body.

VULNERARY — Used in healing wounds.

Spells

The casting of spells is old and a very basic aspect of paganism. Like more formal ceremonial rituals, spells serve to focus the mind and the will on the magical task to be accomplished. One can go through all of the motions of a complex spell but lack the requisite ability to direct the natural forces and the spell will be useless. This may be a good thing in view of the proliferation of books on the market today telling us how to cast spells to achieve all manner of cosmic and earthly goodies. Some of these spells are being published here not because they necessarily get good results, but merely because they are entertaining to read. Some of them, particularly the love spells, are better read and left unpracticed because of their attempts to influence the consciousness of another person. If one wants to do a love spell and not violate any ethical standards, rather than trying to attract a particular person, it is better to project an image of the one's self attractive to various members of the opposite sex.

The spells presented here pertain largely to Earth and Earthly matters. Other spells shall be presented in subsequent volumes.

For Good Fortune

Take a little red bag and sew it with red woolen thread. Then take a crumb of bread, salt, a sprig of rue, and some commun —

> This bag I sew for luck for you,
> And also for my family,
> That it may keep by night and day,
> Troubles and illness far away.

Ancient Gypsy Love Spell

This enchantment is best used to win a man who has not requited the feeling of love which the lady holds for him.

In a red vase or pot, plant a small ivy leaf (the ivy carries the idea of constant, ever-growing and reviving love). As the plant is watered, repeat this spell, with eyes closed:

> **As this shrub grows**
> **And as its leaf blows,**
> **Let his love arise for me.**

Thereafter, nurture the plant carefully. If it grows well for you, you will gain the one you love.

Sand Ritual Love Spell

In a box of sand trace the initials of your would-be lover's name in large letters and then, directly over them, your own. Infuse the sand with magic by leaning over and kissing the initials (a kiss is a very potent thing). Then, gather some of the sand of the initials and place it in a small vial. The next time you see your hoped-for admirer, sprinkle some of this sand in his hair (make sure that he is unaware of your actions). The force of this spell would work on his mind and bring him to your side.

Dragon Blood Spell (Voodoo Folklore)

Dragon Blood is the name of a red extract (gum resin) from a tree native to the Malay Archipelago. In solid stick form it is carried on the person for luck. To get rid of curses, hexes, and crossed conditions, it is burned in powder form at midnight for seven nights. This is done near an open window.

Marjoram Spell (Medieval Folklore)

Majoram was prized as a charm for defeating evil forces, and said to be a love charm if added to food. It is an herb of Venus, planet of love. If used against evil it had to be placed in each room of the house and renewed each month.

Wart Spells (English Folklore)

Ancient spells of England regarding the removal of warts by magical means are:

1. Rub the warts with a piece of bacon, cut a hole in an ash tree, put the bacon in it. Warts will transfer to the tree.
2. Touch each wart with a pea. Wrap each pea in a piece of paper which is then buried in moist ground. The warts were said to disappear as the peas decayed.
3. Prick each wart and put three drops of blood on elder herb, and this is buried like the pea for the same purpose.

The Cauldron or Mill Dance

This is chanted two or three times in order to generate power in working a ritual. Everyone should join their right hands in the center of the circle and walk around, gaining momentum and chanting faster.

> Air breathe and air blow.
> Make the mill of magic go,
> Work the mill for which we pray,
> Io dia ha he yay.
>
> Fire flame and fire burn,
> Make the mill of magic turn,

Work the will for which we pray,
Io dia ha he yay.

Water heat and water boil,
Make the mill of magic toil,
Work the will for which we pray,
Io dia ha he yay.

Earth without and earth within,
Make the mill of magic spin,
Work the will for which we pray,
Io dia ha he yay

Radiant Health

This spell, properly executed, was supposed to enable a person to attain and maintain radiant perpetual health. Facing the East with arms spread wide, an invocation is said:

Lord God of the Heavens and all above, and all below, I pray Thee to grant me the power to conceive of the Life Fluid, the Life Force, so that I may, with Thy divine help, become a part with it, body and soul. If it shall be Thy divine will, the glorious Life Force shall permeate me and suffuse me, and bring everlasting well-being. Grant me, O Great God, this favor. Amen.

Maintaining the same position the supplicant mentally pictures a force of energy from the Universe sweeping towards him or her. As it arrives, one draws in a deep breath, visualizing and feeling the force being drawn in and down to the solar plexus. As the breath is slowly exhaled, a mental picture is to be formed of this force spreading and flowing either to all parts of the body or to a specific area. This is done over and over again. With practice the mental picture becomes easier to envisage.

Charm of Consecration

> **One for the Window**
> **Two for the Hearth**
> **Three for the wooden Door**
> **Four for the Mill**
> **Five for Jill**
> **Six to make Seven More**
> **X   X   X**
> **Three crosses make**
> **Blessings all.**

This requires a cord for each working pair, or else each person has a single cord to knot.

By knot of one	* – – – – – – – –	*The spell's begun.*
By knot of two	* – – – – – – – *	*It cometh true.*
By knot of three	* * – – – – – – *	*So mote it be.*
By knot of four	* * – – – – – * *	*The open door.*
By knot of five	* * * – – – – * *	*The spell's alive.*
By knot of six	* * * – – – * * *	*The spell is fix.*
By knot of seven	* * * * – – * * *	*The stars of heaven.*
By knot of eight	* * * * – * * * *	*The stroke of fate.*
By knot of nine	* * * * * * * * *	*The thing is mine.*

The Abracadabra Spell

Although this famous charm was recorded in the third century by the Romans, it would seem to trace its origin all the way back to the Chaldeans of Babylonia. The Chaldean phrase translates almost exactly into the English pronunciation, and refers to a fever disappearing like the word. The patient said the whole name on the first line, and progressively dropped one letter as he pronounced each line in turn until no letters were left. As this was done, the fever was supposed to diminish. Also the charm was to be written on a piece of parchment which was to be put on a cord and hung from about the sick person's neck.

ABRACADABRA
ABRACADABR
ABRACADAB
ABRACADA
ABRACAD
ABRACA
ABRAC
ABRA
ABR
AB
A

To make things flourish and grow, do a spell during the waxing moon — from the first day of the new moon to the first day of the Full Moon. At this time work for an increase of anything, or to diminish something.

To decrease anything do a spell during the waning period of the moon. This is a good time to get rid of any bad situation, including illness.

To put a stop to anything irksome, choose the second day of the Full Moon.

Use silver and white to establish a link with the Moon.

Anti-War Spell

Take a news clipping of the war and roll it into a cylinder. Tie the clipping with a black thread. Place the paper into a green glass bottle with no writing on the outside and stop the bottle with a cork. Taking the bottle to a river or ocean place a symbol on the glass with waterproof ink. Then cast the bottle into the water (outgoing tide, waning moon) and remain at the spot until the bottle has disappeared from view. This ritual should add some power

Mugwort Spell (Medieval Witchcraft)

Prophecy could be accomplished with Mugwort according to this ancient belief. Known as a "Witch herb" it was used as an incense by crystal gazers. This was due to its leaning to the north as it grows, which gave rise to the idea that it had strong magnetic and supernatural powers. To cause prophetic dreams, the Mugwort was placed in a cloth bag and kept under the pillow at night. Witches offered it as a charm spell to keep a traveller from tiring. Mugwort can also be consumed as a tea and is said to induce clairvoyance.

Ritual

Ritual is the systematic working procedure dedicated to achieve a particular aim or effect on individuals or groups. It is usually a practice that when repeated, with the same intention, dedication, working methods, time and sacramental techniques produce the effects or affects.

Ritual is learned by practice and observation, but it has become increasingly necessary to list methods for building a ritual, plus samples of ritual and hopefully, to construct practical operations for themselves in a private capacity and perhaps they will leave something for those who follow.

Basic Points

A ritual must have intention. That is, there must be a purpose for the ceremony, even if it be simple devotion. The purpose must be understood ahead of the time of working and not change during the course of the work. Next, there must be method. Any work must not be performed haphazardly. This does not mean perfection of performance, but simply no flouncing around. The Priest, Priestess, or ritual leader must know what he or she is doing, and move steadily toward that purpose using whatever method has been agreed upon, not changing that method in the middle of the stream.

Mood is also very important. One works on many levels in ritual, for we live on all planes simultaneously. It is the inner reponse to the outer action that affects the changes caused by what we term magic. This inner or subconscious change reflects directly upon our outer physical plane self and directly and indirectly upon the self that exists on the other planes. Therefore it is necessary for emotional control so that concentration and meditation can effectively be worked.

It is necessary to hold attention for long periods of time on one subject, and mixed emotions hinder this. In methods such as healing, it is necessary to direct your feelings to the person you are working for, and if these feelings do not produce the proper or desired result, harm rather than healing results. Also, when directing powers from other levels, the wrong mood can call adverse vibrations to you, or your inner self will interpret the result in the wrong fashion and damage could occur. Therefore, it is necessary to approach ritual in a frame of mind that will help, not hinder your work. It is best to begin thinking about the ceremony days before the actual working. It is necessary to avoid people a few hours before the ritual. Immerse yourself in the emotion that is to accompany your work. Walking out of doors helps to open oneself to the vastness of the universe. Taking a bath helps to effect the feeling of purity. Music certainly helps to calm the emotions, or excite them if that is the way of the ritual. Music is one of the prime factors that can be an aid to ritual construction. Music can change or create mood. Music is the method we can use to adequately instruct the innerself of the attitudes we wish to obtain in ritual worship.

The approach to all these methods is, of course, through the mind. We are psychological beings. It must be recognized that all of our realizations, all of our perceptions, are based upon the action and reaction of the inner and outer minds. In the methods described above, all of the action occurs through the mental channels.

All of these methods use in some way the same methods of repetetive wordage. The idea is to implant the emotion through the use of sound, color and through vibration into the inner mind, affecting the symbols there, effecting the results desired. Other tools, such as smell (incense), feel (tools), and the interaction of mind to mind response used in groups are useful to help the individual more easily perform the task he sets for himself.

Ritual Outline

There are many methods of working ritual and the methods depend upon the type of work to be done. However, there is a simple outline that one can follow in constructing one's own ritual. It is easily followed and complete enough to become the form for almost any ritual.

1. Establish intention
2. Construct ritual outline.
3. Set up temple.
4. Cast Circle.
5. Invoke Higher Forces.
6. Invoke God and Goddess.
7. Perform work.
8. Thanksgiving.
9. Close Circle.
10. Reconstruct Temple.

1. One must have a reason for any ritual work. This reason can be simple worship, but there must be purpose in everything that one does when contacting the divine forces. The first step must be to establish the reason for the intended work. The intention must be clearcut, with a beginning and ending point.
2. The next step after deciding the work of what you are going to do is to establish the HOW. You must know what beings and forces are to be invoked or evoked. The tables of correspondences listing God names, incense, mantrams, etc., must be used as part of the routine exercises. The color scale of the operation must be determined from the table of correspondences and efficiently used. All of these steps are

necessary to contact the desired points within the reference of western occultism.

3. The temple is set up next. This includes vestments, tools, candles, altar, in fact the entire temple. Even if the ritual is to be performed in a closet or the mind, the temple must be prepared. Robing is included in the preparation of the temple.
4. The Circle is next, cast in whatever manner is selected. For sample and deeper explanation see "The Circle."
5. It is necessary to open channels to the Lord God of all the Unmanifest existence. Even if we do not comprehend its existence, we must recognize its existence. At the beginning of ritual this is an invocation to the higher self or greater god forces existing in man. See the chapter on "Invocation" and sample of ritual for examples.
6. Next we invoke the God and Goddess, the manifested Godhead.
7. Work is defined as the project to be accomplished by the ritual.
8. We must return that which we have taken. We must balance the forces with which we work. Thanksgiving can be simple "Thank You," or can establish eucharistic ritual.
9. See the section on closing the Circle.
10. Reconstruct the temple by removing the tools used for special work to their usual place of rest. Then unrobe.

There are many variations from this sample, but the basic pattern must remain the same. The Universe exists as a balanced polarity and we who tamper with its existence and use its natural laws, must maintain that balance. The results of unbalanced forces are far reaching, and as students of the occult we must be ever dedicated to their maintenance.

Rituals

After consideration we are attaching a varied assortment of sample ritual material. Most of this is written to enable one to work them alone, but may easily be adopted to group work. All of the attached may be adequately understood and operated from the information available here. They are simple enough that their form may be easily copied for additional ritual composed by the student himself.

The dedication and first degree initiation are self explanatory. These are included after some hesitation, but perhaps the good outweighs the bad. It must be understood that initiation and dedication is a serious thing, and never to be undertaken lightly. They interact upon the physical body as well as the mental and spiritual, and if undertaken unprepared could cause some damage to the student.

The Qabalistic Cross

A simple ritual gesture should be made before and after occult meditation work. The appropriate one for our purpose is the Qabalistic Cross:

1. Touch the forehead with the right hand and say

Ateh.

2. Touch the breast and say

Malkuth.

3. Touch the right shoulder and say

Ve Geburah.

4. Touch the left shoulder and say

Ve Gedulah.

5. Clasp the hands on the breast and say

Le Olahm, Amen.

The Christian form of this is embodied in the words "For Thine is the Kingdom, the Power and the Glory, forever, Amen." This, as it appears at the end of the Lord's Prayer is sometimes put forward as the reason for believing Christ to have been a Qabalist. Tempting though this supposition may be to Qabalists, it cannot be proved by this evidence for the phrase was a liturgical interpolation some centuries after Christ's death.

To touch the brow and say "Ateh" (Thou) is to affirm the existence not only of the Architect, Creator and Sustainer of the Universe, but also of the Godhead within, the Spark of Divine Fire, or Monad, which is the center and architect, creator and sustainer of one's own being. The top of a brilliant white cross should be visualized as starting from just above the top of the head.

On bringing the hand down to the breast, the vertical arm of the cross should be imagined to extend down to the floor beneath the feet. Obviously it is impossible to trace such a cross exactly without considerable physical contortion, so the touching of the brow and the breast are symbolic indications of intention and actual visualization.

The touching of the breast and saying "Malkuth" (The Kingdom) affirms one's faith and rightful position in the Kingdom of Earth, both macrocosmically and microcosmically, which is to say, both as a being operating upon this physical planet created by the Father of Humanity, and also in a physical vehicle or body created by one's own True Self.

The touching of each shoulder in turn accompanies the visualization of the horizontal arm of the cross, also in brilliant white light. Again, this should extend just beyond the periphery of the physical body.

The translation of the words Geburah and Gedulah causes their intention to become perhaps less apparent — which is why it is better to use the original Hebrew, or as the early Church Fathers did, to substitute the words "Power" and "Glory," which are the translations of the titles of the 7th and 8th Sephiroth on the Tree, which are diametrically opposite Geburah and Gedulah, the 5th and 4th Sephiroth, and in a way, lower reflections of them.

Without becoming involved in technicalities beyond our present state of understanding, the point that is intended in the drawing of the horizontal bar of the Qabalistic Cross is the affirmation of the underlying principle of the whole manifest universe, macrocosmic and microcosmic. This principle is the Principle of Polarity.

This simply means that all things are the result of the equilibration of opposites in complementary action. The atom is the result of opposing electrical forces of particles, the child is the result of the union of opposite sexes — and so on.

"Le Olahm," which we translate as "the world or universe" and also as "forever" indicates a concept midway between these two approximate translations. One could perhaps render it as "the Eternal Beingness" and what is here affirmed is a faith in and acceptance of the whole sum of creation and uncreation, which is, was, and is to come.

"Amen" is the final personal affirmation, "So be it." It can come after a greater or lesser pause and marks the end of the formula and the cessation of active visualization, though the effects of this exercise may be felt for some time after.

Outline of the Elemental Eucharist

The elemental eucharist or the elemental thanksgiving, or even the eucharistic sacrifice, is an act of faith on the part of the worker. It is an assumption of the elements into the self of the worker, and the offering of the self to the lords of the universe in thanksgiving of the knowledge of the light. The eucharist is the recognition of the manifested God and Goddess through their elements represented by the four quarters.

The ceremony itself is a very simple one. Fire, a smell of some sort, usually incense, wine, bread and salt, the universal representatives of the four elements are concentrated by offering them to the Kings of four quarters, and asking the elements of the four quarters to descend into the offering. To the east, incense (air); to the south, a candle (fire); to the west, wind (water) and to the north bread and salt (earth). The dedicated elements are then brought to the high priestess near the altar, for distribution. If no priestess is present, then the priest or celebrant himself distributes the elements.

She says:

> **Smell with me this incense, the symbol of air**

(all smell)

> **Feel the warmth of this candle, the symbol of fire**

(all feel the heat from the candle)

> **Eat with me this bread and salt the symbol of the earth**

(all eat)

> **And finally, drink with me this wine, the symbol of water.**

(all drink, and all of the bread and wine must be consumed

All stand a moment in meditation.
This ceremony can be quite beautiful if the dedicants

invoke the elements eloquently. It is a moving ritual. Almost immediately the student feels some identity with the four quarters, and after some study of the elements and their meaning a feeling of rapture quickly evolves. It must be performed slowly and with dignity, without conversation, and with undivided attention directed to the concentration and consumption.

Dedication

When an inquirer is found to be suitable for the Craft, but not yet ready for admission to a coven, a ceremony called "Dedication" may be performed. The purpose of this Rite is to call the attention of the Lady and the Horned God to the individual, and specifically to his desire to enter the Craft.

Dedication is not a formal or rigorous Rite. It may be performed at any time a Priestess or Priest desires, and when the candidate feels ready to receive it. Initially the occasion for the ceremony is solemn, as the candidate should feel that in being dedicated he is undertaking an obligation to do all that is in his power to make his way into the Craft and full participation in it. After the ritual ends, the occasion is joyous as the candidate has now started upon the road which will lead him to the Craft, and has acknowledged his beginning steps toward full participation.

All that is needed to perform the Dedication is a candle, although incense may also be used if desired. The symbolism of the light is in this instance rather obvious. Light, or knowledge, is at the end of the road on which the candidate is embarking. In being dedicated, the candidate acknowledges that he is making a start on that road.

The candidate must either ask for dedication, or he may be told that he may be dedicated if he wishes. He must, of course, agree to the dedication for it to be effective, and the Rite must be done by a member of the Priesthood of the opposite sex to the candidate, although an intermediary can serve if necessary.

Once the candle is lit it must be left to burn out, symbolizing that once the candidate is dedicated she or he will live out this lifetime in the dedicated state.

The lunar phase is not important, but waxing is somewhat better than waning.

Dedication has the result of impressing on the newcomer the seriousness of his undertaking the study of the Craft. Dedication of a candidate on his first inquiry into the Craft is unusual, and should not be undertaken foolishly. Usually it is better to see a candidate for a few times before the Rite of Dedication is performed. The conditions for Dedication are not restrictive.

The candidate should read through the Dedication completely before the ritual begins.

☆ ☆ ☆

The Outline of the Dedication

Candle and candle-holder are at hand. They are placed on a low table at which the candidate may kneel. Copies of the Rite are also placed on the table so that the candidate may read from them.

PRIEST(ESS): **Do you wish to be dedicated**
To the Gods and the Craft,
That you may learn of them
And that you may join the Craft of
the Wise,
When you are ready?

CANDIDATE: **I do.**
Blessed be my eyes
That have seen this day.

PRIEST(ESS): **Blessed be thine eyes.**

CANDIDATE: **Blessed be my ears**
That hear thy voice.

PRIEST(ESS): **Blessed be thine ears.**

CANDIDATE: **Blessed be my mouth**
That it may speak of thy blessings.

PRIEST(ESS): **Blessed be thy mouth.**

CANDIDATE: **Blessed be my feet**
That have led me in these ways.

PRIEST(ESS): **Blessed be thy feet.**

The candidate kneels in front of the table, and lights the candle.

CANDIDATE: **O Mother of All,**
Creatress of all living,
O Father of the woodlands,
Will you teach   (name)
That I may learn of thee
And become wise in the love of the
**   Gods**
Strong in the aid of man,
Learned in thy arts,
And skillful in thy ways.

PRIEST(ESS): **Beloved,**
Do you pledge yourself to the
**   Goddess**
To love her
And to the Horned God
To honor him?

CANDIDATE: **Gladly do I pledge myself**
To the Goddess, to love her
And to the Horned God, to honor
**   him.**

PRIEST(ESS):   Beloved,
Do you pledge yourself to keep silent
Of what you shall learn
And to respect that which is taught
   you?

CANDIDATE: Gladly do I so pledge myself
To the Goddess, to love her
And to the Horned God, to honor
   him,
To keep silent of what I shall learn
And to respect that which is taught
   me.

PRIEST(ESS):   Then hear the charge of the Great
   Mother,
Called by all names of power among
   men,
Before whose altars all the world
Has approached in reverence:

I am the Eternal Goddess
Yet I demand no sacrifice . . .
Rather I give to those who honor me.
Yet I charge you, that if you would be
   mine
And follow in my ways,
You shall gather yourselves,
Once at each full moon
And give worship to me . . . to your
   Queen.
Each of you must recognize me
And look at me,
Lest you forget from whom you
   come

And to whom you are called.
If you would be mine you must honor
    my charge,
For those things which I have made
    law
May be dissolved by no man.

Shall you obey this charge?

CANDIDATE: Gladly shall I obey
The charge of the Goddess.
I pledge myself to the Goddess, to
    love her
And to the Horned God, to honor
    him,
To keep silent of what I shall learn
And to respect that which is taught
    me.

PRIEST(ESS):   Then you shall be taught to be wise,
That in the fullness of time
You shall count yourself
Among those who serve the Gods,
Among those who belong to the
    Craft,
Among those who are called the
    Mighty Dead.

Let thy life, and the life to come
Be in the service
Of our Noble Lady.

CANDIDATE: Blessed be this time that marks my
    life.
That I shall ever after be a child of
    the Gods,

That I shall learn of them
And embrace them as my own.

Priest or priestess makes the Sign of the Pentacle in blessing the candidate, and says:

> May the blessing of our Gracious Lady
> and of Her hearty Consort
> Go ever with thee.

The candidate arises and is usually kissed and congratulated by the Priest(ess) and then by the other initiates in attendance.

First Level Initiation — Pagan Way

The candidates sit in meditation in a room not far from the temple. They are blindfolded and robed.

The Priest and Priestess cast the Circle in the usual fashion. The Priestess invokes the God and the Goddess:

> Descend upon us this night in all your radiant power.
> We invoke your aid in this rite we perform in your name,
> Welcoming those who seek your worship
> Into our midsts.

All visualize the God and Goddess descending into the Circle.

PRIEST(ESS):   **Blessed Be those within the Circle.**
Cleanse thy heart and mind,
That only truth be spoken,
That only truth be heard.

Priestess and Priest bless members.
Candidates are brought to the edge of the Circle.
The Priestess then opens the Circle, and blesses the candidates with the Pentagram of fire and says:

Do you seek the Way?
Will you serve the Goddess and give
reverence to the God?
Will you guard that which is shown
you from the unworthy?

CANDIDATES: **I do and shall.**

PRIESTESS: **Then I ask you into this sacred Circle**
in this holy place
Be you ever aware that from this day
your life must be
To the service of the Gods.

Your soul has wandered in darkness,
seeking the light
Of knowledge.
You have entered upon a path where
you shall find the light.

Eko, Eko, Azarak
Eko, Eko, Zomelak
Eko, Eko, Gananas
Eko, Eko, Arada.

The Priestess places the sword at the candidate's throat and says:

> In the name of the Lady and those covenanted to
> Her, I place this threefold charge upon you:
> To know the Goddess and the God: To love the
> Goddess and her Consort, and through the knowledge
> Of the Way, to serve the ancient ones.
>
> Do you, (name) Freely accept this charge?

Initiates are unblindfolded and given the sign of the Pentacle with wand or sword by the Priest.

PRIESTESS: I welcome you to the way of the ancient ones,
To the fold of the old religions, into the house
Of the pagans. Hear ye our charges:

Your first duty is that which we have said above, but there is another law and it is:

Do what thou wilt, so long as you hurt no other.
Do you accept this, and swear to abide by it?

INITIATES: We do.

PRIESTESS: **Then I welcome you into our midst.**

Five-fold kiss, to each. Return to larger Circle.

☆ ☆ ☆

North
West   East
South

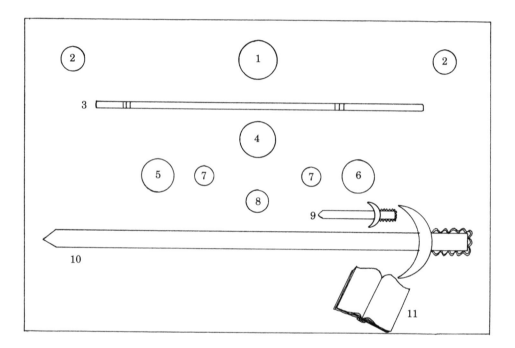

1. Goddess Statue

2. Candles of Illumination

3. Wand

4. Earth — Dish of Bread or Cookies

5. Cup of Wine

6. Censer

7. Water (left) Salt (right)

8. Fire Candle

9. Athame (H.Priestess')

10. Sword

11. Pagan Way Book of Shadows

The Circle

By definition the magic Circle implies a confining space, a limitation, separating that which is within from that which is without.

It is a limiting factor as well as a binding factor. The Magician limits himself to the attainment of a specific end, and that no longer is he in the world of changes and a blind wanderer without aim, objective or aspirations. Within the Circle, complete control exists. It is a built environment dedicated to a specific purpose.

The Circle is the symbol of the infinite.

It also represents the astral sphere of the worker, or the individual consciousness. The Circle in which one encloses himself represents his particular cosmos. In this way, the Circle expands the ego of the magician, for the worker builds a miniature universe within the Circle, one that is slowly built, symbolically in most cases, filled with invocations and instruments that call to the inner mind the work that is to be done at the particular time. Slowly the man initiates himself within this Circle and he begins to understand the world without.

Casting of the Circle

In order to begin any ritual circumstance a Circle must be cast. The Circle is generally nine feet in diameter. If possible, a permanent Circle should be painted or drawn on the floor. Where this cannot be done, the Circle can be laid out with rope or string, or else this can be done visually. The Circle is always formed clockwise or deosil, as opposed to counterclockwise or widdershins.

The Circle is cast clockwise for invocation, counterclockwise for banishing. It is begun in the east in all systems. To each of the directions is assigned the particular point allocated to the element of that sphere:

East, Air; South, Fire; West, Water; North, Earth

Guardian and divine names are sometimes painted on the floor, but these names are but an outward sign for the real work that is done on the astral plane, where the actual Circle or temple is cast. Before casting, the area is banished of unwanted spirits, and invoked for those elements desired for the operation.

The Circle is not to protect one from undesired elements, but simply to set a spatial limit within which spiritual work may proceed unmolested and without fear of intrusion by unwanted forces. (A Circle may be used for protection of this sort, but is another type of Circle and not the same as cast for magical operation). One must not at any time ever enter magical work with fear in one's heart, for you will fail, and perhaps results such as obsession will occur.

One does not always have a temple available, so the Magic Circle transforms an ordinary room into something else, and to most efforts is a temple. The physical difference between a Magical Circle and a temple is that the Circle is two dimensional and the second is three. In a temple, a permanent Circle is usually inscribed upon the floor, but still the magician uses his imagination to build the temple on the other plane.

The Circle represents the whole of man (that is, of oneself) and the whole of the Universe.

The Magic Circle (temporary) should be cast of chalk.

Four candles are set up around the Circle, colored for the elements.

East, Orange; South, Red; West, Blue, North, Brown or Green.

Prior to the actual forming of the Circle the consecration of salt and water must be done. This consists of touching the water with the Athame and saying:

I exorcise thee, O creature of water,
That thou cast out from thee all the
Impurities and uncleanlinesses of the
Spirits of the world of phantasm.

Next, the salt is touched with the Athame and the following is said:

Blessing be upon this creature of
    salt.
Let all malignancy and hindrances
    be
Cast forth hencefrom, and let all
    good
Enter herein. Wherefore I bless thee
That thou mayest aid me.

Then pour the salt into the water and mix with the
Athame.

The Circle is traced with the ceremonial sword. Next,
take the salt water and sprinkle this with the help of the
sword, going around the Circle. Then carry the censer
around the Circle. The next step is to walk around it with
the sword, once more tracing the Circle, saying:

I conjure thee O Circle of power that
Thou beist a boundary between the
Worlds of men and the realms of the
Mighty Ones. A guardian and a
Protection that shall preserve and
Contain the power which we shall
Raise within thee, wherefore do I
Bless thee and consecrate thee.

Then pick up the sword and extend the right arm saying:

I summon, stir, and call thee up,
Ye Mighty Ones of the East to
Attend our rites and guard the
Circle.

Then trace an invoking pentagram. Repeat this step for
directions South, West, and North. Once again face East,
right arm extended, and say nothing, but merely trace an
additional invoking pentagram.

All gather within the Circle. A moment of meditation contemplating the work to progress. The censer is lit and carried around the Circle. All are then purified. Light the candles. The Priestess invokes the God and Goddess. Four elemental kings are invoked by all, led by ranking members:

East — Yod He Vau He
South — Adonai
West — Eheieh
North — Agla

After the work has been completed, the Circle must again be uncast. This is done by the Priestess who thanks the Lord and the Lady for attending.

In the Craft, the Circle becomes a bounding force — one that so contains the power raised to be utilized for the work in progress.

It is the words and intention used to cast the physical Circle and mental direction for the astral Circle that caused the binding element or the protection element. In the mind, one must visualize a wall or force separating those within the Circle from those without.

So, naturally, it must follow that concentration and visualization exercise must precede the first actual attempts to build the Magical Circle.

Personal Protection

Unfortunately, in the world today, and also in the past, exists those who tend to align themselves with the negative forces of existence. Fortunately, the true black magician is as hard to find as one who practices white magic. There is, however, another area of life that exists as a much greater influence upon us than most of us imagine. This is the use of the type of ability most people today term telepathy, or mind power. It is the same thing Christians and related religions call the power of prayer. In the occult world, it is sometimes called thought forms, elementals and other related terms. By definition it is the transference of thoughts from one mind to another by the various means at hand.

Have you ever had an overwhelming desire to do something, perform some act that is normally outside your regular activity? Have you ever wished for something to happen, and then it did? Did you ever want someone to help you perhaps fall in love with you, give you a promotion or money, and then it did occur? With just a little introspection we all know this is particularly a normal daily occurrence in one form or another. In the business world it is called getting together and tossing a thought around, and coming up with an answer, or more likely the answer from someone else in the form of performance. A recent Wall Street Journal article stated more company presidents and officers have this ability than most other people.

Did it ever occur to you that this thought control could be used to control your wishes and actions, even to the point of controlling you against your will? In most cases, the person controlled does not even know that he is controlled, but simply wished to give them money, love or help in some form or other.

The Circle we have been discussing is a method of preventing this control and protecting oneself from the undesired influence of others.

There are two important times when one is open to mind control. The first, naturally, is when asleep, when your conscious mind is resting, and the second is during the awake hours when the mind drifts or day dreams, or when your conscious mind no longer has full control.

The description is the clue to the solution — protection of the inner consciousness from intruding vibrations.

Protection When Awake

When your mind is active the chances of control are much less than when you are inactive. Therefore, day dreaming and like activities should be curtailed, except when within the Circle of protection that I shall shortly describe.

The first step — do not allow the mind to drift. The next step is to build into one's normal personality, the protection of a body shield. This is accomplished by what we can simply term the hardening of the auric shell — deflecting unwanted outside thoughts, and also preventing others from reading your own emotions, a process not usually wise. As an example, think of that what they want you to think. Sometimes, when you are talking to others, they suddenly eliminate any emotional contact you may have established and seem suddenly hard to understand. This is the thing we want to cultivate in ourselves and be able to produce it at will, and hold this protective effort as long as necessary.

136

Method 1

Sit in a chair in a room alone. Relax completely becoming aware of your body. Expand your consciousness outside of your body into the electromagnetic field that surrounds yourself. You know this is accomplished by a feeling of mental tingling that seems outside of your body. Your mind is then in your auric sphere. Surround yourself with a gray wall, extending above your body two feet or so. Contain your entire emotional experience within the shield. Hold it as long as possible then relax, and begin again. This is building a wall of sorts in your aura. Imagine the wall to have the capacity to expel any unwanted thoughts or emotions of others. This shield must be accompanied with complete mental control. Fear is the mind killer, opening the inner-self as it tries to reject the unwanted emotions. Practice this exercise when it is built into you, and then it will remain and need only to be renewed occasionally. Surround yourself with this shield whenever you feel others may be attracting or intruding upon your private self.

Method 2

To be used when more protection is needed. In this method, we will incorporate the method above, plus add an incantation or mantrum that fills the outer mind with protective vibrations. This process is to occupy the entire self with the obsession of protection and attract to oneself powers that will give strength and protection themselves. This should be used only in extreme cases when the need is great. Build the body shield. Next, call upon the four great powers of the four quarters:

> East — **Raphael** *(Ra-fay-el)*
> West — **Gabriel** *(Ga-bree-el)*
> South — **Michael** *(Me-kay-al)*
> North — **Auriel** *(Au-re-al)*

The east will be your front, the west your back, the south on your right, the north on your left. Visualize the powers as great angelic figures standing in these directions; facing away from your body. Vibrate the names clockwise over and over, vocally if necessary, until the attack has diminished.

Protection When Asleep

Sleep is the time when we are most open to psychic attack or telepathic suggestion. For protection the best method is to sleep within the Magic Circle. It is not necessary to construct as complete a circle as previously described, unless attack is feared, but a simple type of pentagram ritual is recommended.

After you are in bed for the evening and when you are ready for sleep, form a pentagram (banishing) in the east, and pierce the center with the God Name YOD HE VAU HE. These pentagrams are formed out of white light. From one of the points move a white bank of light to the south, form another figure, and vibrate the diety ADONAI. Continue the process to the west, vibrating EHEIH, and then to the north, intoning AGLA. Continue the bank of light back to the first pentagram. You are then surrounded with four pentagrams in each of the four quarters, connected with a continuous band of light. Next, from the north pentagram move the band of light overhead to the pentagram in the south. Continue the bank of light under you, back to the pentagram of the north, thus surrounding yourself with another circle of light. Perform the same task from the east to the west, overhead, and then continue on under yourself back to the station of the east. Now you are surrounded with three circles and four pentagrams. This affords complete protection, but must be performed each evening before sleep.

Suggested Reading List

THE OLD RELIGION

Buckland, R.: Witchcraft From The Inside
Buckland, R.: Witchcraft The Religion
Buckland, R.: Witchcraft, Ancient and Modern
Buckland, R.: The Tree
Buczynski: Witchcraft Fact Book
Donovan, Frank: Never On A Broomstick
Farrar, Stewart: What Witches Do
Huson, Paul: Mastering Witchcraft
Gardner, Gerald: The Meaning Of Witchcraft
Gardner, Gerald: Witchcraft Today
Glass, Justine: Witchcraft, The 6th Sense
Harrison, Michael: The Roots of Witchcraft
Hughes, P.: Witchcraft
Huson, Paul: Mastering Witchcraft
Leek, Sybil: Diary Of A Witch
Leek, Sybil: The Complete Art of Witchcraft
Leland, Godfrey: Aradia
Lethbridge, T.C.: Witches
Martello, Leo: Witchcraft The Old Religion
Michelet, Jules: Satanism And Witchcraft
Murray, Margaret: The God Of The Witches
Murray, Margaret: The Witch-Cult In Western Europe
Neuman, Erich: The Great Mother
Ross: Pagan Celtic Britain
Valiente, Doreen: Where Witchcraft Lives
Valiente, Doreen: ABC of Witchcraft
Wentz: Fairy Faith In Celtic Countries
Whiz, Griz: The Witches Ladder

FICTION AND POETRY

Achad: XXXI Hymns To The Star Goddess
Anderson, Victor: Thorns Of The Blood Rose
Crowley: Moonchild
Crowley: Diary Of A Drug Fiend
Garrar, Stewart: The Twelve Maidens
Fortune: The Demon Lover
Fortune: The Goat Foot God
Fortune: Moon Magic
Fortune: The Sea Priestess
Fortune: The Winged Bull

Fortune: The Secrets of Dr. Tavener
Gardner, Gerald: High Magic's Aid
Renault: The Bull From The Sea
Renault: The King Must Die
Shea, R. & Wilson, R.: Illuminatus (Tril.)
Tolkien, J.R.: The Hobbit
Tolkien, J.R.: The Lord Of The Rings (Tril.)
Walton, E.: The Children of Llyr
Walton, E.: The Isle Of The Mighty
Walton, E.: Prince Of Anwen
Walton, E.: The Song Of Rhiannon

MAGIC

Bardon, Franz: Initiation Into Hermetics
Bardon, Franz: The Practice of Magical Evocation (Advanced)
Bardon, Franz: The Key To The True Quabbalah (Advanced)
Brennan, J.H.: Astral Doorways
Brenna, J.H.: Experimental Magic
Butler, W.E.: Magic, Its Ritual, Power and Purpose
Conway, David: Magic: An Occult Primer
Crowley, Aleister: Book IV (Advanced)
Crowley, Aleister: The Book Of The Law (Advanced)
Crowley, Aleister: Magick In Theory And Practice (Advanced)
Crowley, Aleister: Magick Without Tears (Advanced)
Crowley, Aleister: Liber Aleph (Advanced)
Crowley, Aleister: 777 (Advanced)
Denning & Phillips: The Magical Philosophy (Advanced)
Edwards: Dare To Make Magic
Fortune, Dion: Applies Magic
Fortune, Dion: Aspects of Occultism
Fortune, Dion: Avalon Of The Heart
Fortune, Dion: The Esoteric Philosophy Of Love And Marriage
Fortune, Dion: The Mystical Qabalah
Fortune, Dion: Practical Occultism In Daily Life
Fortune, Dion: Psychic Self Defense
Fortune, Dion: Sane Occultism
Fortune, Dion: Through The Gates Of Death
Fortune, Dion: The Training and Work Of The Initiate
Gray, William: The Office Of The Holy Tree Of Life
Gray, William: Simplified Guide To The Holy Tree Of Life
Gray, William: Inner Traditions Of Magic
Gray, William: The Ladder of Lights
Gray, William: Magical Ritual Methods
Knight, Gareth: Occult Exercises And Practices
Knight, Gareth: The Practice of Ritual Magic
Long, Max Freedom: The Secret Science Behind Miracles
Ophiel: The Art and Practice of Astral Projection
Ophiel: The Art and Practice Of Clairvoyance

Ophiel: The Art And Practice of Caballa Magic
Ophiel: The Art and Practice of Creative Visualization
Ophiel: The Art and Practice of the Occult
Ophiel: The Art and Practice of Talismanic Magic
Ophiel: The Oracle of Fortuna
Regardie, Israel: The Art of True Healing
Regardie, Israel: The Art and Meaning of Magic
Regardie, Israel: A Garden of Pomegranates
Regardie, Israel: The Golden Dawn (Advanced)
Regardie, Israel: The Middle Pillar
Regardie, Israel: The Tree of Life (Advanced)
Regardie, Israel: Twelve Steps to Spiritual Enlightenment
Skinner, S. & King, F.: The Techniques of High Magic
Torrens, R. G.: The Inner Teachings Of The Golden Dawn

MYTHOLOGY

Frazer, Sir J.G.: The Golden Bough
Gayley, Charles M.: Classic Myths
Graves, Robert: The White Goddess
Guest, Charlotte (Trans): The Mabinogian
Hamilton, Edith: Mythology
Harding, M., Esther: Woman's Mysteries
Larousse Encyclopedia Of Mythology
Mac Cana: Celtic Mythology

TAROT

Butler, Bill: Dictionary of the Tarot
Case, Paul: The Tarot
Crowley, Aleister: Tarot Divination
Crowley, Aleister: The Book of Thoth
Gray, Eden: A Complete Guide to the Tarot
Huson, Paul: The Devil's Picturebook
Nordic, Rolla: The Tarot Shows The Path
Roberts, Richard: Tarot and You

MISC.

Brown, Joseph: The Sacred Pipe
Buckland, R.: Practical Candle Burning
Culpepers Complete Herbal
Cerminara, Gina: Many Mansions
Davidson: A Dictionary Of Angels
Grieve, M.: A Modern Herbal

Huson, Paul: Mastering Herbalism
Jung, C.G.: Man and His Symbols
Lady Sara: Candle Magic
Leek, Sybil: Reincarnation The Second Chance
Maltz, Maxwell: Psycho-Cybernetics
Man, Myth And Magic: Volumes 1-24
Martello, Leo: How To Prevent Psychic Blackmail
Meyer: The Herbalist
Neuman, Erich.: The origins and History of Consciousness
Powell, A.E.: The Astral Body
Powell, A.E.: The Causal Body
Powell, A.E.: The Etheric Double
Powell, A.E.: The Mental Body
Powell, A.E.: The Solar System
Scully.: Treasury of American Herbs
Wilhelm, R. & Baynes, C. (trans.).: The I Ching